Am I Missing Something . . .?

Unpublished Letters to The Daily Telegraph

EDITED BY
IAIN HOLLINGSHEAD

Aurum
Press

First published in Great Britain
2013 by Aurum Press Ltd
74–77 White Lion Street
London N1 9PF
www.aurumpress.co.uk

This edition published in 2015 by Aurum Press Ltd

A catalogue record for this book
is available from the British Library.

ISBN 978 1 78131 556 9

10 9 8 7 6 5 4 3 2 1
2019 2018 2017 2016 2015

Typeset by SX Composing DTP, Rayleigh Essex

Printed and bound by CPI Group (UK) Ltd, Croydon, CR0 4YY

Am I Missing Something . . .?

SIR — I've been reading your latest collection of unpublished readers' letters and I have some suggestions. Firstly, please can I have the job of reading all the letters when they first arrive? I would, of course, work for nothing and pay all my own expenses.

Secondly, could you start a franchise campaign whereby only people who contribute to the letters section of the paper are allowed to vote in general elections?

Brian Hill
Winnersh, Berkshire

CONTENTS

INTRODUCTION

Now that these books are in their fifth year, some of my more cynical friends have taken to asking if I make up any of the wonderful letters which appear in them. I'm never sure whether to be offended that they think I'd stoop to such subterfuge or flattered that they consider me capable of inventing such a range of wise and waggish opinions. The truth is that a decent letter to the editor of the *Telegraph* is almost impossible to fake. The genuine article can be spotted at 100 paces — a unique combination of well-turned wit and whimsy, worldliness and world-weariness, learning and light-heartedness, which always leaves you wondering just how firmly the tongue is pressed against the cheek this time.

You might expect a pedestrian letter-writer to have produced some mundane opinions this year on topics such as Wimbledon, the Pope, gay marriage, equine lasagne, the rise of Ukip and the birth of the future king (or the birth of Pippa Middleton's nephew, as some picture editors would no doubt rather caption it). Only *Telegraph* correspondents would write to share the fact that their gardener thought they were watching pornography when he heard the shrieks of the ladies' semi-final; that *Farage* means something

crude in Malay; that the Pope's resignation
statement contained a split infinitive or that the
Duchess of Cambridge should get a move on as the
interminable speculation was spoiling the Ashes.
And who knew that so many readers – not to
mention their mothers – had met Sir Patrick
Moore?

Our correspondents never cease to surprise and
delight. It is true that some hail from Tunbridge
Wells and that some, on occasion, show disgust. Yet
they're much more likely to be baffled, bemused,
furious or downright outrageous. Many are
hilariously unreserved when it comes to revealing
the eccentric details of their private lives. All share
an ability to use language not just as a means of
communication, but as a tool for play. Innovative
signs-offs this year include 'yours filthily', 'yours in
a tizz' (over Stephen Fry, inevitably), and, perhaps
my favourite, '*Cruda viridisque senectus* indeed!'.

The letters are so well – and so warmly – written
that it is a pleasure to return to their writers'
company every summer and see what they've made
of the year's events. It certainly provides an excellent
lesson in the geography of the United Kingdom.
In the unlikely event that I ever wanted to go
on Mastermind, I would choose 'letter-writers'
villages and their counties' as my esoteric specialist
subject. After a few years' study I can, without
too many passes, match Norton Juxta Twycross to

Warwickshire, Smeeton Westerby to Leicestershire, Rhosllanerchrugog to Wrexham (though I'm not sure I could spell it) and perhaps most apt, Yelling to Cambridgeshire.

To all our correspondents, whether in London SW3 or Hoghton Bottoms, Lancashire, my grateful thanks, as well as to Christopher Howse, Caroline Buckland, Matt Pritchett, Graham Coster and everyone at Aurum. I'm especially grateful to Arthur House, who has expertly mined many thousands of emails, sifting the wheat from the even better wheat, and without whom the book would not have been possible.

Am I missing anything . . .? Ah yes, a title for next year. I've recently enjoyed some entertaining correspondence with readers sharing their suggestions. One problem is that every time I think we've found a good one, I check on Amazon and, worryingly, it's already been taken by Jeremy Clarkson. This year, after writing the first paragraph of the introduction, I thought I'd stumbled upon a corker: *You Couldn't Make it Up.* And you know what? You couldn't — it's already been used by the illustrious combination of Richard Littlejohn and Jeremy Kyle.

Back to you. I can't wait to see what you come up with next year.

Iain Hollingshead
London SW1
August 2013

FAMILY LIFE
AND
TRIBULATIONS

WHAM, BAM, THANK YOU, SON

SIR — I am a 78-year-old widower and wanted some company during my latter years, so I looked at several dating agencies. Not wanting 'wham, bam, thank you, ma'am', I decided on the *Telegraph* Dating Service.

I had a couple of dates for which there was no chemistry. The next one, however, was totally different and very exciting. I informed my son of the result. The next time he visited he said, 'Dad, I have brought these for you' and handed me two condoms.

I replied to the effect that I had previously undergone a prostate operation and did not require them.

He said: 'Dad, get up to date, you don't need them for that, but in today's world you have to be very wary of STDs.'

Later I was working in my garden and suddenly became somewhat peeved that he thought I would require only two when he knew I was away for several days with this younger lady. So I called and asked him why.

He immediately burst into laughter and replied, 'Well, just in case you lost one.'

John Ford
Ipswich, Suffolk

PS Please publish this as it makes me laugh every time I think about it, but under a pseudonym, otherwise I will be in deep trouble.

SIR — A friend of mine, an 80-year-old widow, tells me she receives birth control pills from the NHS as they help her sleep. Curious about this hitherto unknown side effect, I enquired how they work. She said she grinds them up and puts them in her granddaughter's orange juice.

Nicholas Betts-Green
Woodbridge, Suffolk

SIR — I don't know if any of your readers have ever played reverse strip Scrabble: everybody sits naked, but if you make a five-letter word you can put on a piece of your clothing.

That, however, was years ago and now at the age of 67, we play with the traditional rules.

Martin Thurston
Liphook, Surrey

SIR — Your item today, 'Really, we want cuddles' is most apt. I am nearly 80 and my partner is not far behind. I can assure you that we greatly enjoy our cuddles and have lots of them.

W. George Preston
Southampton

SIR — I saw two women in the local supermarket pick up one of the tabloid papers. I overheard one say to the other, 'My husband and I have been having the same sex for years and I promise you it is nothing to get excited about.'

I am still laughing to myself, because it really does sum it all up.

Jean Ratcliff
Barnet, Hertfordshire

THE PLEASURE OF BEING A LABOURER'S MATE

SIR — Your correspondent wonders how a widower should introduce a new lady friend. As a widow, I married for a second time a widower who worked as an architect and surveyor until the age of 82. It was my great pleasure to be able to act as his assistant when he travelled, but all the more so to be introduced to clients and colleagues alike as 'my hod-carrier'.

Sybil Hampton
Bradley, Hampshire

SIR — I found, 'This is my new bird' broke down a few barriers.

Patrick Wroe
Felixstowe, Suffolk

SIR — My husband introduces me as 'My current wife'. We have been married for 25 years.

Jean Baveystock
Bentworth, Hampshire

SIR — As my wife and I approach our ruby wedding next year one of my sons asked me for tips for an enduring marriage. My answer was simple: 'Agree with her when she's wrong and apologise when you're right.'

Tim Lemon
Irby, Wirral

SIR — I speak for only 10 minutes every day to my wife, while she speaks for 16 hours to me, followed by seven hours, 50 minutes snoring loudly.

> **G.F. Zurcher**
> Lindfield, West Sussex

SIR — I have always found silence to be the most effective answer when arguing with a clever woman.

> **Albert Smetham**
> York

SIR — On waking in the morning, the first words I utter are, 'I'm sorry'. It sets the tone for the day.

> **Mick Richards**
> Llanfair Waterdine, Shropshire

SIR — Much depends on the tone of, 'Yes, dear'. My wife has eight different ways of saying it, six of them threatening. We have been happily married for many years.

> **John Preston Bell**
> Meopham, Kent

SIR — When I grew a beard in middle life I asked my wife to give an opinion of the finished job. She replied: 'It's like adultery but without the hassle.'

I took this as a vote in favour, but thought it better not to ask her about the experience on which she based this view.

Quentin de la Bedoyere
London SW19

WHEN WE'RE 220

SIR – My wife recently underwent a serious operation and her sister flew in from Arizona to nurse her during her recovery. An elderly lady who lives opposite my home informed neighbours that I had a 'blonde dolly bird' living with me while my wife was away.

My wife is 70, her sister 73 and I am 77.

Should I remonstrate with the lady, or thank her for the compliment?

Terry Justice
Chadwell Heath, Essex

SIR – Why does the body's clock appear to go haywire in our latter years? I spend half the night trying to sleep, then half the day trying to stay awake.

Neil Kershaw
Royton, Lancashire

SIR — Does anyone else think that pensioners, at risk in this prolonged heat wave, should be given an air-conditioning allowance?

Jane Denton
Hornsea, East Yorkshire

SIR — Has old age finally caught up with me? Today, while out shopping with my wife, I looked down to see I was dressed in beige clothing; I bemoaned the fact that department stores fail to supply chairs for bored husbands; and to cap it all, on my return home, I repaired a pair of spectacles with Sellotape, à la Jack Duckworth, the barman from *Coronation Street*.

Michael Cattell
Mollington, Cheshire

SIR — I am a female of 92 and have recently started wearing jeans, finding them very comfortable. I ignore the common German saying, 'Seen from the back, high school. Seen from the front, museum.'

B.C.
Taunton, Somerset

SIR — Don't people realise the only place to wear denim is in the garden, garage or while creosoting the fence; jeans are nothing more than overalls.

Some of the jeans worn to functions I would use only to wipe spilt oil from a garage floor.

Jim Pickering
Crimond, Aberdeenshire

SIR – The age of a man wearing jeans does not trouble me a bit. What I do heartily dislike is the modern trend of wearing jeans with a formal suit jacket. It seems neither fish nor fowl and looks, in my eyes, patently ridiculous.

Patricia Naxton
Caversham, Berkshire

BRING YOUR OWN BELT

SIR – My invitation to our 50th wedding anniversary party with a request that gentlemen should wear ties has been met with hoots of derision from the family and I am waiting to see how many turn up with their ties around their waists holding up their trousers.

John Forrest
Fetcham, Surrey

SIR – I find it almost impossible to buy a pair of trousers which reach my waist so that I can usefully employ a belt. They seem to be built for builders, so as to expose varying amounts of bottom.

I am told this is fashion.

Chris Strong
St Mary Bourne, Hampshire

SIR — Our nearest small town is blessed with a priceless relic from a bygone age: a Gentleman's Outfitters.

My trousers all have turn-ups and buttons for braces, but my waistcoats remain totally unbuttoned due to excess girth. I regularly use a napkin clip and have designed and made several for use by ladies, using two crocodile clips and a small chain.

The braces sometimes cause problems at airports with Portuguese security staff, who charmingly refer to them as *suspendarios*, which makes them feel exotic.

I have not worn socks for nearly 20 years and am considered slightly eccentric, but by golly, I am comfortable.

David Pimblett
Horbury, West Yorkshire

SIR — I have a shirt with no fewer than four buttons on the cuff. Can any reader beat that?

Peter de Snoo
Perranwell, Cornwall

SIR – May I congratulate Boris Johnson for
discovering a use for the middle button on
his jackets.

John Ley-Morgan
Weston-super-Mare, Somerset

SIR – I can accept that a vain and masculine Henry
VIII living in the modern age may well, as your
picture suggests, be tempted by a hair transplant and
false tan, but a jacket with buttons on the left and
breast pocket on the right? Never!

Michael B. Smith
London SE13

SIR – I have to confess to not previously being
aware of the existence of Anne Hathaway (I'd
always thought she was Shakespeare's mother).
However, the picture of her in today's *Telegraph*
caused me considerable anxiety. For several
seconds I thought that she had stolen my
Marks & Spencer vest.

Nigel Peacock
Llanbedr y Cennin, Conwy

SIR – Having just discovered what onesies are, I
realise that, in the 1940s, I was 70 years ahead of
fashion, except that we called them 'siren suits'.

Even Winston Churchill had one, though I don't suppose his was made from an old coat, as was mine.

Dorothy Preston
Batley, West Yorkshire

SIR — It was great to see Antonia de Sancha smoking and dressed in what appears to be an animal fur; how very counter-cultural. I make a point of hugging women who smoke — since giving up seven years ago it still has a powerful allure.

Michael Willis
Stirling, Fife

SIR — It can hardly be a surprise to the owners of Holkham beach that people, when naked, feel like sex and are less likely to be uninhibited about it. Isn't that one of the main reasons we started wearing clothes in the first place — a means of controlling our baser instincts?

D.McC.
London W14

HUSBAND FOR HIRE PURCHASE

SIR — Your letter-writer reminds us of the benefits of joining up with fellow shoppers to obtain a

discount. Can I suggest a similar tip? Go to a
well-known DIY store on a Wednesday and take
an 'over 60' with you to obtain the 10 per cent
pensioners' discount.

Now that my husband has reached this magic age,
I am considering hiring him out.

Moira H. Brodie
Bourton, Wiltshire

SIR – My husband embarrasses me every time
we leave a shop that has the sign, 'Thank you for
shopping here, please call again' by calling out loud,
'Again'.

Pam Soper
Clevedon, Somerset

SIR – My wife and I went to a London departmental
store to obtain a replacement light bulb after it
stopped working after just nine months.

When asked possible reasons for the short life of
the bulb, the assistant replied that they do not like
being switched on and off.

Have we missed something?

Raymond Kite
Keston, Kent

SIR — I have just bought a new pair of scissors. There is a problem though, as I need a pair of scissors to cut the plastic fastenings.

Jan Chapman
Fulwood, Lancashire

SIR — I am a retired RAF Engineering Officer and now a househusband. Am I alone in thinking that OXO cubes are difficult to unwrap?

Dave Alsop
Churchdown, Gloucestershire

SIR — Our local Tesco displays its wide range of lavatory rolls on the aisle directly opposite the baked beans. Could this be a wind up?

Ken Milne
Southport, Merseyside

SIR — Why do supermarkets think I need two of everything? I am not a pig.

Frazer Spence
Canterbury, Kent

CORDON NOIRE CUISINE

SIR — In earlier years my dear mother had a propensity to overcook food. She was known as a 'Cordon Noire' chef, who utilised the smoke alarm as a timer.

Jonathan Sinclair
London NW4

SIR — In 1950s colonial Kenya, my mother discovered the kitchen hand cooling the toast slices between his toes.

Marion Ansell
Underriver, Kent

SIR — Following a clear-out of our refrigerator I have just enjoyed a bowl of Fridge Soup. My wife was prepared to declare: Jerusalem artichokes, roast parsnips, roast beetroot, pheasant stir-fry, chicken and ham stock, a slice of lemon, the rinsings from a pot of mango chutney and a dash of home-made chilli sherry. It was quite delicious but, sadly, can never be repeated.

S.K.
Tilton on the Hill, Leicestershire

SIR – While walking my dog I picked up some rubbish at the side of the road. It was an empty packet of reduced fat Weight Watchers Hot Chilli Tortillas. Enough said?

James Griffin
Hayling Island, Hampshire

DELIGHTFULLY EQUINE LASAGNE

SIR – I cannot be the only person who has been both shocked and delighted by the amount of meat to be found in Findus lasagne. I have avoided such products for years, assuming they contained very little meat, and shall now put them back on the menu.

Jason Peacock
Beverley, East Yorkshire

SIR – I was amused to be informed of the Findus horsemeat discovery by the BBC News radio reporter, Mr Furlong.

Adrian Stockwell
Farnham, Surrey

SIR – Does the prevalence of horsemeat in the food chain explain the popularity of Gangnam Style?

Julie Ingerfield
Calne, Wiltshire

SIR – I know we are all concerned about food safety, but I bought my wife a bunch of daffodils today from Sainsbury's, only to find that they were labelled in two separate places: 'Do not eat'.

Peter Rathbone
Macclesfield, Cheshire

SIR – A large sign in my local Tesco proclaims: 'Our whole chickens are 100 per cent British'. What else could they be? If they were only 50 per cent British, where would the other half come from?

Keith Edwards
Tattershall, Lincolnshire

SIR – Imagine my surprise when, finishing our evening meal of supermarket beef burgers yesterday, my wife and I both bounded into the garden and did two fast laps round the perimeter, jumping the garden seat twice. My wife won by a short head.

Geoff Morton
March, Cambridgeshire

SIR – How would Sir like his burger cooked? Rare, medium or good to firm?

Steve Cattell
Hougham, Lincolnshire

SIR – Could my lack of success at the bookies be due to me unwittingly backing horses with cow DNA?

Alan Field
Scarrington, Nottinghamshire

SIR – Following the discovery of Richard III, should archaeologists now consider digging up the local supermarket car park, in an attempt to locate his horse?

James Carver
Dymock, Gloucestershire

SIR – Last Monday you published a letter from one of my contemporaries at Eton. He claimed that, unknown to us, we were fed horsemeat on a regular basis.

I arrived at Eton having been a successful athlete at my prep school. Within two or three months my times for the mile, the hurdles and the steeplechase improved dramatically.

I thought that this was strange. I now know that it

was the horsemeat and not my strict training regime that made this happen.

Tom Barnard
Wareham, Dorset

SIR – Horsemeat in school dinners? No such delicacies in my day.

Tim Silk
Ulwell, Dorset

SIR – Like many of your readers I was pleased to read that Shergar had been found at last. I wonder how long we have to wait until Lord Lucan is revealed, perhaps in a hot dog sausage or a tin of spam. Might we have stumbled across an international racket?

Nigel Foster
East Cowes, Isle of Wight

I'M ON THE HORSE

SIR – Why do people need to be in touch 24/7? Have they all become so insecure? I horse ride alone regularly, so my wife insisted I have a mobile to use in case of emergencies. Anyone requesting the phone's number is told that it doesn't accept incoming calls.

The only emergency so far has been to ask my wife to hold the ice from the gin, as I am going to be late home.

> **Victor J. Llewellyn**
> Hingham, Norfolk

SIR — In an idle moment over the Christmas break I decided to have a coffee in one of the high street coffee shops (I know, 'Traitor!', I hear you cry). A group of youths came in, ordered their coffees, sat at the table and proceeded without any interaction with each other to use their mobiles and iPads to contact other people.

It started me wondering how the youth of today would cope if suddenly there was no electricity, no broadband and no mobile signal. Would they all magically be able to resort to log tables, slide rules, pen and paper, and face-to-face conversations?

> **Mike Haberfield**
> Springfield, Buckinghamshire

SIR — I consider the use of mobile phones at the dining table to be the height of bad manners. It ruins my concentration whilst I am trying to read the *Telegraph*.

> **David R. White**
> Grantham, Lincolnshire

GLASS HALF EMPTY

SIR – An Oxford University study, no doubt carried out at great expense, claims that a daily alcohol limit of one unit would save 4,600 lives a year. A private survey, carried out by myself, at no expense whatsoever, shows that thousands of lives would be saved by imposing a speed limit of 3mph on all roads.

I would suggest that the contingency of either of these limits being implemented is equally remote.

Leonard Macauley
Staining, Lancashire

SIR – If I drink double the recommended amount of alcohol, it is because I am experiencing only half the quality of life I aspire to.

Chris Wood
York

SIR – Dry February is better than Dry January. It is shorter, even in leap years.

Bruce Rushworth
Radcliffe on Trent, Nottinghamshire

SIR – I did it! Now for my local, the Bermuda Triangle, and its four cask ale hand pumps, ranging

from right to left in ascending order of strength.
I intend to travel in that direction, starting at 5pm
prompt. In a responsible manner, of course.

Tim Palmer
Poole, Dorset

SIR — Some 65 years ago, when I first started
drinking, an experienced drinking colleague gave
me the following advice: 'When you first enter a
bar, take a good look at the barmaids. They will only
improve from that moment onwards.'

Peter Durrant
Long Stratton, Norfolk

THE BIRDS, THE BEES AND THE DT

SIR — In response to my children's enquiring
minds on the finer aspects of human reproduction,
I answered each relevant question as it arose,
enthusiastically embellishing the tale with simple
illustrations to aid their understanding.

My husband was somewhat puzzled one evening
to find the margins of his beloved *Daily Telegraph*
graffitied in a seemingly pornographic manner. I
explained that it was the only paper to hand.

The children and I still rate the *Telegraph* highly in

their understanding of the 'birds and the bees' and remember their lesson with hilarity and fondness.

Teresa Robson
Knightcote, Warwickshire

SIR – Thirty years ago I sent my husband and 12-year-old son on a long walk with instructions to my husband to give the boy the 'birds and the bees' talk. Two hours later husband and son returned. When I asked how the talk had gone my husband replied, 'Well, I don't think he learned much, but I certainly did.'

M.S.
Newbury, Berkshire

SIR – While taking in my washing I found a large, dead bumble bee in my knickers. My husband remarked, 'What a way to go.' I'm not sure the bumble bee would agree.

K.W.
Sissinghurst, Kent

KEEPING ABREAST OF
SCIENTIFIC DISCOVERY

SIR — I don't suppose Professor Rouillon is the first man to study women's breasts, but he is surely the first to decide for us that bras are useless. He should try running for the bus with no bra and two coconut-sized protuberances bouncing about.

R.B.
Collicello di Amelia, Umbria, Italy

SIR — Is it possible that Professor Rouillon's study of 355 women's breasts may be culturally biased? In the interests of verification, I am prepared to conduct a similar British survey. As I am now retired, I believe I could even knock a couple of years off the 15 that it took the good professor to complete his labours.

Paul Rathkey
Shipston on Stour, Warwickshire

SIR — You report that *Tatler* has 'raised eyebrows with a feature on "best society breasts"'. If the magazine can cover aristocratic balls, why can they not uncover aristocratic breasts?

Ramji Abinashi
Amersham, Buckinghamshire

SIR — I have been reading a girl's magazine.
It appears that the way to a man's heart is through
the acquisition of a pert little posterior,
demonstrated by stunt bottoms belonging
to a bevy of incredibly rich models living in
America, and achieved by 'lunging, squatting and
killer kickbacks'.

However, a beautiful bottom may only be half the
story, especially if one considers the article 'fit and
fierce', which involves heavy vamping in ill-fitting
under-crackers while rock climbing in 'look and
lust' killer heels.

At which point a whole new dimension
presents itself, heralded by 'great sex for
grown-ups' (as if there were any other kind),
which goes a long way to convince the reader
that 'love exercising' cuts more mustard when
enjoyed in the company of a blood orange sorbet
with champagne.

Anyone for tennis?

J.G.D.
Withnell, Cheshire

WEATHER SCAPEGOATS

SIR — Am I alone in wondering whether the
responsibility for the current cold weather lies with

teachers? Has it all been especially arranged in order for them to have time off?

Norna Taylor
St Neot, Cornwall

SIR — The reason for our cold spring is obvious: the earth is slowing down. Noah died aged 950, yet Abraham, 2,000 years later, lived until only 175.

The Romans understood well that our years were getting longer and added two new months to compensate, naming them after the illustrious Caesars: Julius and Augustus. Today it's time to add another month. I suggest we call it Boris.

John Ingram
Sevenoaks, Kent

SIR — Almost all the photographs of the winter weather have a dog and a walker in them. Some are featured in more than one publication. Are they paid by syndicate agencies to provide human (and canine) interest? Or do they arrange for a friend with a camera to accompany them so they can have their moment of fame?

Clive Godber
Kirk Ella, East Yorkshire

SIR — A mere puff of a 50mph wind destroys a
£250,000, 80-foot wind turbine. What use are
they? We used to have much stronger, sea breezes
sweeping across the rugby pitch when I was a lad in
Weston-super-Mare, but I could still stand up and
generate heat at the same time.

Mike Haberfield
Milton Keynes, Buckinghamshire

SIR — Is it too simplistic to think that one answer
to relieve the flooding problem is to make our
rivers deeper?

Kevin Platt
Walsall, West Midlands

SIR — Friday May 3, 9.01pm, London SW11: first
mosquito of the summer, successfully despatched
with today's *Telegraph*.

Nicholas Sherriff
London SW11

SIR — Could a law be passed to prohibit people with
tattoos from stripping off during periods of hot
weather? Some of the sights I saw today must have
breached my human rights. And the men were just
as bad.

John Frankel
Kingsclere, Berkshire

SIR – The recent sunny weather reminded me that years ago we had to pay to see a tattooed lady; now we can see dozens free of charge.

Tony Cowan
Elgin, Moray

SIR – Heard in my local supermarket today: 'I'll do that when the weather gets back to normal.'

Chris Cole
Maesbrook, Shropshire

SIR – The recent warm weather has brought out a new English euphemism, 'You're looking well.' Translated, this means, 'You've been sunbathing in the garden while I've been stuck in the office all week.'

Graham Masterton
Tadworth, Surrey

THE VET WILL SEE YOU NOW

SIR – Some years ago my wife had the nail of one of her big toes removed in hospital. Sadly the wound turned septic, resulting in three visits a week to our doctor's surgery, all to no avail.

After several weeks I decided to cover the toe liberally with the Wound Powder provided by my vet for our Cocker Spaniel. This resulted in a complete cure in a couple of weeks.

The vet was delighted at our success, but sadly I chickened out of telling the doctor.

Alec Wood
Hoghton Bottoms, Lancashire

SIR – I am reminded of my Welsh farming friends and rugby enthusiasts, who wax lyrical about the benefits obtained by applying peppermint udder cream for all sports injuries.

It's worth a try: it smells good and it comes in a large container.

Diane Huntingford
Tonbridge, Kent

SIR – I am considering having my husband neutered; our local vet assures me that he is very experienced in these matters.

Patricia Grimrod-Smythe
Ingbirchworth, South Yorkshire

SIR – I am blessed with such good health that if my doctor were to pass me in the street, he wouldn't know me from Adam. Yesterday he knew me well enough to sign my passport application and relieve me of £30.

G.E.
Norfolk

SIR – My wife died nearly seven years ago. Today, in the post, she received an invitation to a health screening. Is this a record?

Chris Spencer
Reading, Berkshire

SIR – What a relief that the mid-Staffordshire NHS report was not published before the Olympics opening ceremony.

Ian Hamilton Fazey
Liverpool

SIR – It's good to read that Andrew Marr has made a full recovery. Pity he never heard my old House Master's advice: 'If you are fit, to take exercise is pointless. If you are unfit, to take exercise is dangerous.'

Timothy Dewey
Kelston, Somerset

SIR – You print a report about a young lady who can't stop hiccupping. When I was 14, back in 1947, I was in the Royal Berkshire hospital in Reading. In the next bed was a 'man of the road' who had the same problem.

The registrar on the ward was a Persian. The first time he saw the man he told him to stick out his tongue. He then got a towel and caught hold of his tongue and pulled for a few seconds.

The hiccuping stopped immediately and didn't come back.

J.V. Woods
Gobowen, Shropshire

SIR — You report a link between salad dressing and prostate cancer survival. Sadly your article omits to say to which part of the anatomy the salad dressing should be applied and for how long.

My wife says (so it must be true) that broccoli is another preventative but, sadly, does not know whether it should be raw or frozen. Neither does she know where it should be applied.

Perhaps a broccoli floret covered with salad cream would be the most effective preventative medicine?

Robert Shaw
Knowle, West Midlands

IMPERFECT CHRISTMAS PRESENTS

SIR — Am I alone in wondering how advertisers can tell what I require for my 'perfect' Christmas?

Andrew Blake
Shalbourne, Wiltshire

SIR – In my email box this Christmas morning was a thoughtful gift from British Gas: my latest bill, which, joy of joys, I can view online.

Delivery was at 4.45 am, which by my calculation must have been about 10 minutes before Santa.

Martin Goodwin
Reading, Berkshire

SIR – Is this a record? The first seven Christmas cards received this year have brought news of:

Two artificial shoulders

One aorta artery operation

One stroke

A move into a care home

A big toe amputation

Bleeding ulcers

Eye cataract surgery

Septicaemia, pneumonia, kidney failure, stroke and prosthesis removal

Aged 94, I certainly count my many blessings.

Group Captain G.H. Everitt (retd)
Torquay, Devon

SIR – I was recently asked if we were going to tip our postman this Christmas. Having given it some thought, we've decided to give him back his rubber bands instead.

J.B.
Sheffield

SIR — First class flight, first class cabin, first class meal — we all know what 'first class' means, until it comes to the Royal Mail. Shouldn't Special Delivery be renamed First Class, First Class renamed Bog Standard, and Second Class renamed Steerage?

Terry Gregory
Heckington, Lincolnshire

SIR — Traditionally, I have always sent a Christmas card to my bank manager. Now I do not have one.

Jeremy Taylor
North Mymms Park, Hertfordshire

SIR — The most Christmassy card we received — Baby Jesus, Mary, Joseph, shepherds, angels and a text from the Bible — is from our Muslim friends.

Marion Frayne
Mawdesley, Lancashire

SIR — My nine-year-old granddaughter was chosen for the role of Mary in her school nativity play recently. On the evening of the performance my daughter shouted upstairs to her, 'Hurry up, you'll be late for your star production.'

Downstairs came the reply: 'I can't hurry; I'm pregnant.'

David R. White
Grantham, Lincolnshire

SIR — My grandson, who lives in the north of England, was listening to 'While Shepherd's Watched Their Flocks by Night'.

'Is it about Newcastle?' he asked his mother.

'No. Why?'

'Because they said, "The Angel of the North came down".'

J. Ganley
Chesterfield, Derbyshire

SIR — The question asked by Judith Woods's daughter about her Great Aunt Phoebe disappearing through the crematorium curtains reminds me of my son at my father's funeral.

As we sat waiting for the first rousing hymn of his Requiem Mass, I explained to Jack, aged five, that that was Grandpa's body in the coffin under the flowers.

He looked at me, looked at the coffin and then back at me.

'But what about his head?' he asked.

Perhaps everyone should have a small child with them at a funeral.

Alice Osmond
Alfrick Pound, Worcestershire

SIR — Having just completed the annual chore of 'undressing' the Christmas tree, I thought I should share a helpful tip with fellow readers.

To avoid the lengthy trail of dried pine needles as you drag your bare tree through the house, place the tree inside a duvet cover. This neatly collects all the needles, as well as providing a secondary use for a used duvet cover after the Christmas guests have left.

Nicky Huntingford
London SW13

FULL NEST SYNDROME

SIR — We have had the pleasure of the family at home over Christmas and are now restoring the house to normality. Out of a number of observations, I wish to remark on two.

On opening the fridge this morning, with a view to deciding what of the edible wreckage was suitable to put on my toast, I came across the following: a carefully rewrapped meat pie from an upmarket retailer with a bite taken out of it; and a plate of butter which had been microwaved, resulting in two icebergs sitting among hardened, completely inaccessible butter.

The pie I despair of, particularly as the family are

in their twenties and thirties; the butter I simply find irritating.

My technique with fridge butter is to slice at a thin angle. My wife, on the other hand, creates a trough in the middle, which I also find irritating as it interrupts my angle-slicing approach.

Am I being unnecessarily pernickety?

Dr B.M.
Pitlochry, Perthshire

SIR – All I want for Christmas is for my grown-up independent children to realise what 'grown up' and 'independent' means; that I no longer have an estate car to be called upon to move their belongings from one rental property to the next; that because I am retired I don't spend hours sitting around waiting to 'furniture delivery sit' to brighten up my day; that when you borrow my drill, I do not have to accompany it and operate it; that you do not use my house as the parcel delivery depot for all your online Christmas shopping; that when you come home for Christmas you do not leave on every light in the house; that we do not have any magic elves to keep replenishing the daily emptied fridge and biscuit tin; and when 'I didn't finish it' finishes a lavatory roll would 'I didn't finish it' please replace it?

Happy Christmas.

M.B.
Bourton, Wiltshire

SIR — I've had my doubts about the mother-in-law. Today my wife received a letter from her. It was blank. Any suggestions as to what the meaning might be?

M.W.
Woodley, Berkshire

SIR — I pray I am never caught short while walking along Rottingdean seafront. The very thought of being seen emerging from one of their 'gender neutral' public lavatories fills me with dread. Worse by far, I should imagine, than walking out of a brothel straight into the arms of the parents of one's fiancée.

Yours, thinking the whole world's gone bloody mad.

Lance Warrington
Northleach, Gloucestershire

COLD SHOULDERING THE COLD CALLERS

SIR — When well into his nineties, my late father regarded dealing with cold callers as a kind of sport and actually looked forward to their calls. His most memorable encounter was with a conservatory salesman, whom he kept on the line for at least 30 minutes.

Yes, he would be very interested in a

conservatory. Yes, he would be very happy to meet the representative as he had a lot of money to spend.

Finally he asked: 'Does it matter that I live in a third-floor flat?'

I still remember him chuckling when he said, 'He hung up on me.'

Lynda Skinner
Worcester Park, Surrey

SIR — When my 87-year-old father receives a cold call asking if he would like double-glazed windows his reply is, 'Hang on, I will go and count them.'

R.H.
Chipnall, Shropshire

SIR — One of my replies is, with a very high-class accent: 'I am Lady Bracknell, his Lordship is down in the stables with the horses. Shall I get him for you?'

No reply.

E.H.
Freshwater Bay, Isle of Wight

SIR — My favourite trick is to say: 'Your call is very important to me, please bear with me for a moment.'

I then leave the telephone next to my computer

speaker playing music for five minutes. When feeling particularly vindictive I have songs available by James Blunt, Chris de Burgh and the Lighthouse Family.

Michael Powell
Tealby, Lincolnshire

SIR — We had a call from someone selling double glazing. When we said we were interested they were so flummoxed they rang off.

John de Lange
London N12

CALLS OF NATURE

SIR — Listening to a beautiful dawn chorus this morning I was reminded of a story my late mother used to tell. On a lovely June evening in the 1930s her boyfriend took her out in his open-top Austin Seven for a run in the countryside. They parked in a secluded leafy lane and my mother said, 'Listen to the sound of that babbling brook.'

On closer inspection it turned out to be a cow relieving itself.

James Logan
Portstewart, Co Londonderry

SIR — May I please help with readers' relations with cows? A cow's sense of smell is much better than its eyesight. If you keep downwind of them, they won't smell you and start getting fidgety.

If they get too close, blow into their noses to discomfort them. This also works for dogs, cats, horses, pigeons, mothers-in-law, door-to-door sales folk and politicians.

Gary Sunbeam
Manchester

SIR — For the past 20-odd years I have written to you and others every time there is a fox incident with the simple information that to prevent foxes entering an urban garden, it is necessary only to get all the little boys of the neighbourhood to wee around the boundary. They cannot believe their luck.

Foxes will not cross human urine. My only regret is that the information came to me too late to save our hens: the fox killed 11 and the 12th died of heart failure.

J.M. Cawthorne
Bury St. Edmunds, Suffolk

SIR — The cocks in my small flock of bantams were all named. They included *Cockalorum*, *Cockofthewalk*,

Cockadoodle and a scruffy yellow Silkie called *Staphlococcus aureus*. Two sibling cocks had different temperaments, one stay at home (*Stopcock*) and the other a wanderer (*Gonococcus*).

All were well mannered, since any tendency to fight or peck led to a change of name and lifestyle to *Cockie-leekie*.

Dr Janna de Vere Green
Beccles, Suffolk

SIR — I am glad to see that my wife and I are not alone in giving visiting peacocks names. We had two that used to come to our garden, resting in the herb beds. They were called *Gavin* and *Darren Peacock*, after the footballers.

In earlier times we had a pair of tortoises called *Lillee* and *Thompson*, in view of their speed across the grass.

P.F.
Elveden, Suffolk

SPORTING TRIUMPH AND DISASTER

THE FOOTBALL PAGES

SIR — Surely it cannot be a coincidence that in *The Daily Telegraph*'s Sport section, after a large number of pages headed 'Football', the next page is often headed 'Sport'? What does this tell us about football?

> **Geoff Crome**
> Cambridge

SIR — As much as I loathe and detest football and everyone associated with it, nevertheless, it was a pleasure to see Sir Alex Ferguson on your front page instead of Helen Mirren.

> **Richard Dancy**
> Farnham, Surrey

SIR — Reading Allison Pearson's article about the Rooneys naming their new baby son Klay, my wife and I speculated that, should there be a further addition to the family, s/he might perhaps be named Konkrete.

> **Phil Walker**
> Hull

SIR — Some time ago, if a footballer scored a goal, his facial expression was one of pride and pleasure.

Why do today's goal scorers display an expression of such anger and hatred?

D. Brian Davies
Aberystwyth

SIR – Am I alone in thinking that today's professional footballers spend more time in their hair salons than they do on their training grounds?

Geoff Morton
March, Cambridgeshire

SIR – There has always been a hooligan element among youths and adolescents, but the individual on the front of *Telegraph* Sport today has grey hair. Don't they ever grow up?

R. Cushing
Bristol

SIR – With regards to punishment for footballers who bite other players, has anyone considered pulling their teeth out?

Christo Scaramanga
Matfield, Kent

IMPROVING THE TRUE BEAUTIFUL GAME

SIR — Rugby at times is the true beautiful game: hard, unselfish slog and skill by forwards leading to flowing exploitation by the backs. As a preparation for life it is exemplary: physical hardship without histrionics, forgiveness afterwards and, above all, self-discipline.

But unless we reduce the number of infringements the game will never live up to its potential. Here's one for consideration: an accidental knock-on is rarely an advantage to the side who commits it, so why penalise it?

D.W.
Stockport

SIR — Just about every game in the Six Nations was marred by props losing their grip on their opposite number's shirt. Is it not possible for some kind of pocket or flap to be built into the props' shirts to expedite firm, legal binding?

Brian Farmer
Chelmsford, Essex

SIR – The recent Six Nations must have been the most dreary since its inception. Maverick and pedantic refereeing, periods that made the Eton wall game look interesting and enough big hits to make even the most ardent NFL fan salivate.

Where was the artistry, the side step, the dummy, the adroit kick ahead?

For the television pundit the whole series was ruined by the verbal diarrhoea of the commentators, particularly the wittering of Jonathan Edwards. When will someone advise them to shut up?

Christopher Downs
Goodrich, Herefordshire

SIR – How is it, I wonder, that the singer leading our National Anthem believes she has licence to sing it incorrectly, with the last two notes raised into a shrill, unwanted crescendo, an octave too high, reverberating round the ground and going out on television around the world?

It precedes a game played with a ball. Somebody should give the producer a couple so that he demands a correct rendition.

Mike Higham
St Albans, Hertfordshire

SIR – The half-wits from the RFU who agreed to England taking the field at Twickenham last Saturday dressed like Barbie dolls should identify themselves by wearing purple in public for ever more.

J.P.
Suckley, Worcestershire

SIR – Perhaps the reason for England changing from their usual white shirt to purple is because the person responsible for laundering the England rugby kit can, like the rest of us, no longer find a washing liquid that can get mud stains out.

Ginny Hudson
Swanmore, Hampshire

SIR – When I played rugby, our team would impose severe sanctions on those deemed to be self-centred prima donnas. I can recommend a traditional remedy for Chris Ashton, involving Deep Heat and a temporarily curtailed domestic life.

David Loxton
Sherborne, Dorset

BOAT RACE REPEAT

SIR – In 2004 you ran the story, 'Foul language and cry of foul play as clash of oars mars Boat Race'. Surely the better headline for this year's Boat Race should have been: 'Yet another BBC repeat'?

Sandra Miles-Taylor
St Albans, Hertfordshire

SIR – A cox's cry is not always intended to be offensive. I recall many years ago, in a restricted part of a Head of the River race, the cox of a boat level with us demanding of our crew, 'Water, cox, water', to which our cox shouted back, 'Water yourself'.

Dr Frank Beavington
Ryarsh, Kent

PORTRAIT OF DORIAN BECKHAM'S RETIREMENT

SIR – Matthew Norman's article on David Beckham compared him to Oscar Wilde's Dorian Gray, 'though without the grotesque portrait in the attack [sic]'.

Football-mad proof readers should be wary of

The Ballad of Reading's Goal, *Lady Windermere's Fans* and *The Importance of Bending like Earnest*.

Keith MacInnes
London SW19

SIR – Two years ago, when working in a remote part of Belize, I asked my taxi driver if he had ever been to England. He answered 'No'. I asked if he had met anyone English before. No. I asked if he had heard of anyone English.

'Yes,' he said. 'The Queen and David Beckham.'

David J. Powell
Ashley Heath, Hampshire

SIR – As much as I admire David Beckham as an ambassador for our country, I admire even more the men from 617 squadron who breached the dams in Germany 70 years ago.

Surely, today of all days, you could have shown a picture of the Lancaster passing over the dam at Derwent on the front of your newspaper instead of David Beckham.

P.W.
Marshfield, Wiltshire

OLYMPIC LEG-ACIES

SIR — What a wonderful television programme the *BBC Sports Personality of the Year* was. I had always wondered what Jessica Ennis looked like with her clothes on.

Jonathan Hewitt
Bonn, Germany

FEMALE GOLFERS IN THE PINK

SIR — Dame Jacqueline Wilson says that boys will not read books with pink covers. I find that neither will grown men play with pink golf balls. In fact, if they see one lying on the course they will give it a wide berth and inform the nearest lady of its presence.

I always play with pink golf balls. This way my stock has hardly diminished over several years.

Liz Wheeldon
Seaton, Devon

SIR — Players using mobile phones on golf courses should have them confiscated, placed on a pink tee and driven with a 10.5-degree driver.

G.M.
Newport, Shropshire

AUSTRALIA'S REPUTATION BURNT TO ASHES

SIR – An Australian, Ashton Agar, sweetly says sorry to his mother for failing to score a century on his magnificent and modest Ashes debut. An Englishman, Stuart Broad, unshaven and brazen, refuses to do the gentlemanly thing and walk and tweets our Wimbledon champion: 'Don't really follow tennis but well done Andy Murray on the quality of your Mrs.'

And finally, Australia graciously accept defeat on a controversial decision.

It's just not cricket.

Lesley Thompson
Lavenham, Suffolk

SIR – This is no good. Michael Clarke is too nice.

Elizabeth Bellamy
Grimsby, Lincolnshire

SIR – Watching the antics of the England cricket team when they get a wicket – and particularly when they win a match – makes me wonder where dignity in winning went.

Commodore C.M.J.C.
Montaigu de Quercy, Midi-Pyrénées, France

SIR — Whenever England win at cricket why do you insist on showing a picture of a tattooed, beer-swilling South African?

R. McGrogan
Wallasey, Merseyside

SIR — The widespread decline in Australian sporting success is remarkable. Perhaps this is a result of the country's economic success and consequent rise in living standards; the 'good life' is taking its toll and too many shrimps are now being thrown on the barbie.

Paul Strong
Claxby, Lincolnshire

SIR — What I want to know is who changed the start day of the Ashes from a Thursday to a Wednesday? Today I went to a great deal of trouble setting up the radio and beers in the potting shed, as well as arranging a girly cream tea tomorrow for the wife, only to find that some idiot had moved the start day. I have now missed the first 14 wickets of this long anticipated Test series

Yours not amused,
R.W.
Dorchester, Dorset

SW19-ENDERS

SIR — Why would anyone queue for three hours at Wimbledon to watch two women shouting at each other for another three hours? You may as well watch *EastEnders*.

Jim Wilkinson
Grimsby, Lincolnshire

SIR — Wimbledon fortnight never fails to stir up childhood memories of lengthy family debates over the suggestion that since a game of tennis is decided on the very last point, one need not bother playing any of the others.

Jimmy Jewell
London W1

SIR — Why hasn't that girl who screams been hobdayed? What would have happened if Fred Truman had made such a horrific noise at Lord's every time he bowled?

Edward Wilkinson
Ashford-in-the-Water, Derbyshire

SIR – One possibility is that they are faking their first service.

Frank Tomlin
Billericay, Essex

SIR – I was watching the ladies' tennis match between Sharapova and De Brito, complete with agonised, competitive caterwauling. Through the open garden door, looking unusually sheepish, stepped our gardener. He confessed later that he'd been most relieved to see the green grass of Wimbledon on our screen. From his position amongst the roses he was convinced that Mrs Z and I were watching a porn film.

Zog Ziegler
Haw Bridge, Gloucestershire

ARISE, ST ANDY?

SIR – In the light of Sunday's miracle at Wimbledon, why stop at a knighthood for Andy Murray? Might not canonisation be more appropriate? It seems to be all the rage and Saint Andrew has a certain ring to it.

John Rees
London W14

SIR – I wonder how 'Sir Andrew has two challenges remaining' would sound.

Barbara Hickman
Sheffield

SIR – If Mr Murray receives a knighthood for his Wimbledon win, Leigh Halfpenny, the wonderful Lions fullback, should be awarded at least an earldom.

Charles Nunn
Upton, Wirral

SIR – Will the All England Club now be renamed the All British Club?

John Lederhose
London N21

SIR – I demand a referendum on whether or not Andy Murray should be knighted.

Bruce Chalmers
Goring-by-Sea, West Sussex

SIR – I think Murray deserves a knighthood for putting up with his mother.

Leslie Watson
Swansea

SIR – Have you noticed that since Andy Murray won Wimbledon, it has not rained? Last year when he lost, if I remember correctly, it rained for 40 days.

Edward K. Howell
Swansea

SIR – I am not at all surprised by Murray's win. After all, the date was 7/7, it was 77 years since we have had such a victory and my car's milometer read 77,777.

Caroline Chaffe
Southborough, Kent

SIR – After the great Wimbledon final I risked a joke with my wife. I said: 'Imagine a sensational headline in the *Telegraph* next week: "Murray fails drugs test".'
    She was not amused.

Chris James
Abergele, Conwy

SIR – In 1966 my wife and I were at Wembley to see England win the World Cup. Today, nearly half a century later, we were at Wimbledon to watch Andy Murray. I wonder just how small a group we are members of.

Terry and Margaret Emery
Harrow, Middlesex

SIR — Murray triumphs at Wimbledon, the British Lions rampant in Australia, Frome leads the Tour de France. Meanwhile, the football headlines include an alleged sex assault in Cornwall and a referee beheaded in Brazil.

Christopher Bean
London SE3

SIR — Amid all the well-deserved hullabaloo following Andy Murray's historic victory, it was your front page picture of the lad outside Number 10 that caught my eye. With no obvious bows in his shoe laces, how does he keep them tight?

Robert Warner
West Woodhay, Berkshire

SIR — Is it too much to hope that some of Andy Murray's winnings will be spent on new razor blades?

Tony Allen
East Bergholt, Suffolk

SIR — Tony Blair stated on the *Today* programme that he would 'swap his 10 years as Prime Minister for Murray's Wimbledon crown'.
So would I.

Anthony Gales
Henham, Essex

A YEAR IN
POLITICS

I'M A VOTER, GET ME OUT OF HERE

SIR — If I want to read about the puerile activities 'in the jungle' I shall buy the *Sun*. However, if Nadine Dorries herself is eaten by something, would you promise to hold the front page, please?

Stuart Smith
Houghton, Cambridgeshire

SIR — Should Nadine Dorries really be expelled from the Conservative Party? She comes across as a self-promoting, delusional right-winger with a pathological hatred of David Cameron. So, a typical Tory MP then.

John Boylan
Hatfield, Hertfordshire

SIR — Put Louise Mensch, Nadine Dorries and Sally Bercow in a sack, shake them up, tip them out and you couldn't tell one from the other.

Martin Bazeley
Southwick, Hampshire

SIR — Bercow by name, Bercow by nature. Give him a bit part in the next *Game of Thrones*.

N.P. Scott
Harpenden, Hertfordshire

BLOOD, SWEAT AND TEARS

SIR — I really don't know whether to be more outraged by the behaviour of Eric Joyce MP in the bar at the House of Commons or by the fact that they were holding a karaoke session there. Churchill would be turning in his grave.

David Ellis
Tarves, Aberdeenshire

CRIME AND PUNISHMENT

SIR — You report that prisoners will no longer automatically receive perks such as wearing their own clothes and watching television. I thought the prospect of unlimited daytime television in prison was the greatest deterrent to being sent there.

A.M.B.
London SW11

SIR — A sure-fire way to cause misery and pain among the prison population would be to play endless repeats of last weekend's Reading versus Queens Park Rangers.

A.G. Fox
Bolton

SIR — If second-time inmates were fed only two meals a day, third timers one meal a day, fourth-time prisoners wouldn't last long. Problem solved, Mr Grayling.

Steve Cattell
Hougham, Lincolnshire

SIR — With so many appalling sex crimes recently, should we not be having a debate about castration? Chemical probably, but at least a debate.

A. Hackett-Jones
Glemsford, Suffolk

SIR — You reported a boy being awarded £12,519 having fallen out of a tree on school property. How times have changed: all I got was the cane.

Bill Hodgman
Gosport, Hampshire

SIR — Doubtless this letter will not be published. However, I feel strongly that the only images of the Woolwich murderers that should be seen in the media is that of their execution at dawn today.

Steve Hamilton
Easterton, Wiltshire

ADIEU, ABU QATADA

SIR — What price the right for Abu Qatada's family to enjoy a family life? Desolate and living alone in London they are now being forced to exist on a life of welfare. It is undignified and uncaring, so every effort must be made to restore their dignity and their family life in Jordan.

Even now I am confident that Qatada's British lawyers are — without any expectation of a fee — busily preparing their case for the Court of Human Rights in Strasbourg.

P.H.
Terling, Essex

SIR – Do you think it will be humanly possible for the BBC to get Abu Qatada on 'Thought for the Day' before he buggers off back to Jordan?

Robert Stevenson
Cheltenham, Gloucestershire

SIR – Now that one of the main characters has been deported by Theresa May does this mean that *The Lion King* will have to close?

Peter Nock
Andover, Hampshire

SIR – Now that Abu Qatada is semi-willing to return to Jordan, might he be willing to do many of us a favour and take David Cameron with him?

Patricia Sullivan
Ashley Heath, Hampshire

SINGING CAMERON'S CRITICISMS

SIR – When the camera was on the Prime Minister at the service for the 60th anniversary of the Queen's Coronation, I was surprised – and appalled – to see that he was not taking part in the singing of the hymns.

For me, that says it all.

P.N. Woodward
Little Addington, Northamptonshire

SIR – Am I alone in considering that David Cameron is useless?

B.T.
Fareham, Hampshire

SIR – Of course David Cameron works in his pyjamas. It explains why he is asleep on the job.

D.M. Watkins
Plaxtol, Kent

SIR – David Cameron says he wants to stay until 2020. I think he's more likely to be gone by 8.15pm.

D.C.
London NW11

SIR – Many battles were won on the playing fields of Eton. Presumably, on the days that David Cameron's class was on the playing field, he had a letter from his Mummy.

Ian Beck
Crosby, Cumbria

SIR – In 80 years Eton has educated something in the region of 20,800 boys. I can't see these numbers giving Mr Cameron a majority in the next election.

Linda Mitchell
Scotby, Cumbria

SIR – I wonder if anybody else has removed Eton Mess from their household menus due to its political overtones.

Susan Hardman
Pickering, North Yorkshire

SIR – Much is made of the fact that many in central Government are Old Etonians. Has it escaped notice that many of the powerful women in our lives are Old Marlburians? For example, Samantha Cameron, Frances Osborne and the Middletons.

J.R. (Old Marlburian, but powerless)
Petworth, West Sussex

SIR – Yet again the Prime Minister and his wife are shown on television holding hands like love-struck teenagers. Do they really have to behave like this in the presence of the German Chancellor and her husband?

Jenny Foxall
Malvern, Worcestershire

SIR — I wish to retract my previous letter, just in case you have not already binned it. I did not mean to be personal; Dave is doing his best, I suppose, and I am becoming concerned that I am turning into one of those Greenham Common types in my advancing years.

Mike Haberfield
Springfield, Buckinghamshire

PAYING FOR PORNOGRAPHY

SIR — You quote Claire Perry MP, 'an adviser on pornography to David Cameron'. You mean to say he has an adviser to tell him what to look at and we're paying her salary?

Duncan Rayner
Sunningdale, Berkshire

SIR — It is all very well to rant about removing porn from the internet — it would be as easy to remove wee from a swimming pool.

Jane Cullinan
Padstow, Cornwall

SIR — Predictably, the alarmist nonsense about 14-year-old boys accessing pornography being a cause for 'moral panic' and a 'public health issue' comes from a couple of women, respectively the 'deputy children's commissioner' and David Cameron's 'adviser on pornography'(what frighteningly Orwellian titles!).

I have news for them: they always did. By the age of 14, long before the internet was invented, I supplemented my pocket money by running a private library of naughty pictures and magazines for my schoolfellows. I'm sure every boy in the year had seen them.

Dr Robin Rudd
London W1

SIR — In going through the effects of a deceased relative some years ago, I came across his remarkable collection of 1940s *National Geographics*, with their educational pictures of South Sea Islanders in the garb nature intended. The magazine certainly lived up to its name.

Tony Pay
Bridge of Cally, Perthshire

REDEFINING MARRIAGE JOKES

SIR — You do realise that the gay marriage bill ruins the only joke I can ever remember: Should a married couple be frank and earnest, or should one be a woman?

Jerry Dixon
Hythe, Kent

SIR — Since the advent of gay marriage, at our factory we no longer employ men of child-bearing age.

A.C. Ball
Greenfield, Manchester

SIR — Whatever happened to those clever, artistic, interesting queers of my youth? Now they all want to be boring, middle-class, married couples. What is this world coming to?

David Wiltshire
Bedford

SIR — Gays should be able to marry so they can suffer like the rest of us.

Leslie Watson
Swansea

SIR — Being a devoted husband, as well as a staunch
and active member of the Conservative Party, I'd be
grateful to learn what further changes it will adopt,
especially in regard to monogamy. My wife could do
with a bit more help around the house.

Robert Vincent
Wildhern, Hampshire

SIR — I can't quite work it out: is Mr Cameron a
closet gay or a closet liberal?

P.F.
Wortham, Suffolk

SIR — Looking at our Christmas card list I am not
sure how to address those of our gay friends who
may be marrying next year. So far we have Mr and
Mr, Ms and Ms, Mrs and Mrs and Ms and Mrs. Are
there any other permutations I have missed?

We have a particular dilemma with a sex-change
couple.

Robin Clark
Compton Bassett, Wiltshire

SIR — I sympathise with the noble Lord Hylton
concerning his regret over the loss of the 'fine old
word *gay*'. All is not lost, however. Perhaps he could
replace it with one of the words used (by another

vociferous group) to describe homosexuals, such as *poof, queer, shirt-lifter* or *faggot,* as in, 'We went to a delightful faggoty dance party last night.'

In any event I think he needs to get out more.

Philip Tucker
Brighton

SIR — Would it help if *marriage* were reserved for heterosexual unions and *garriage* for gay unions, whose participants could *garry* and then be *garried*?

Roger Spriggs
Hythe, Hampshire

SIR — I read in your Sunday edition that the Bishop of Buckingham has spoken out on the Church's ban on blessings for homosexual partnerships. There must be a limerick somewhere in there.

Hugh Smorfitt
Tichborne, Hampshire

SIR — Will female bishops preside over gay marriage ceremonies?

P.J. Minns
Frilford, Oxfordshire

SIR – Although I have managed to come to terms with same-sex marriage, there is something much more sinister going on. I refer, of course, to a number of pantomime producers using a man to play the part of Principal Boy. No fishnet tights, no thigh slapping, no concession to tradition. Whatever next, I wonder. The ugly sisters and dame played by women? Not in my lifetime, I sincerely hope.

Timothy St. Ather
London SW13

SIR – The protracted gay marriage debate is certainly keeping the economy off the front pages. Our Prime Minister is brighter than we thought.

W.K. Wood
Bolton, Lancashire

THE GREEN SHOOTS OF INSANITY

SIR – I understand that the definition of insanity is doing the same thing over and over again and expecting a different result. Would someone please alert the Chancellor of the Exchequer?

Pamela Goldsack
Banstead, Surrey

SIR – Tories insist there is no Plan B for the economy. Will there be a Plan BBB instead?

Robert Dobson
Tenterden, Kent

SIR – It was comforting to read that George Osborne said in his Budget review that he has made 'real progress', which is much better than the imaginary kind.

Tim Hubbard
London SW14

SIR – Am I alone in thinking that the photograph of George Osborne exercising in St James's Park last Sunday bears a remarkable likeness to Jeremy Clarkson?

P.H.
Terling, Essex

SIR – This Budget is really encouraging the binge drinkers. Every 250 pints of beer they drink they will save enough to buy another pint.

E. Gould
Orpington, Kent

SIR – In the current climate of austerity should NHS-funded breast enhancements be treated as an investment? Some 20 per cent of future modelling fees could be returned to the NHS.

Alan Beer
Staines, Berkshire

SIR – Am I alone in finding today's lavatory paper incredibly thin? Is this another manifestation of austerity? Are we to retreat to squares of newspaper, which many of us endured in the 1940s?

Bernard Walton
Blairgowrie, Perthshire

SIR – By this morning's post, my wife and I received two identical notifications, in separate envelopes, from NatWest, telling us that they plan to change how often we receive statements for our joint account. This is 'in order to reduce the amount of paper we use'.

These people are our principal wealth creators (I read that in Alex, so it must be true), yet I worry.

Peter Wyton
Longlevens, Gloucestershire

SIR – You report that civil servants waste three
days a year waiting for their computers to boot up.
I find something else to do while I wait for mine;
why can't they?

Ian Beeston
Sandside, Cumbria

SIR – Shopping is not my favourite pastime,
but it was pleasing to see Manchester so busy
yesterday. If everyone spent as much as my wife
did I am confident the economy is well on the
way to recovery.

Simon Clarke
Clitheroe, Lancashire

SIR – What with the upturn in the economy,
Abu Qatada, Andy Murray, the Ashes (hopefully)
and Labour's squabbles, I bet David Cameron is
regretting creating fixed-term Parliaments.

John Tilsiter
Radlett, Hertfordshire

TAX THE BEARDS

SIR – First, a Mansion Tax, now there's talk of a
Bedroom Tax. Why stop there? How about a Beard

Tax? This was first introduced by Henry VIII in
1535 and was graded according to the wearer's
social position. It was then reintroduced by
Elizabeth I who taxed every beard of more than
two weeks' growth.

I commend this idea to the House.

Bruce Chalmers
Goring-by-Sea, West Sussex

A VENTI TAX BILL TO GO

SIR — What a fool I've been! For the past 50 years
I have been labouring under the misapprehension
that the payment of tax was mandatory. Thanks to
Starbucks, I now realise that it is voluntary.
Put me down for a tenner, Mr Osborne,
to cover my liability for the next two years.

Dave I'Anson
Formby, Merseyside

SIR — I've been a great fan of Starbucks for many
years, and have bought coffee from them regularly.
So I was very shocked to learn that they don't make
a profit in the UK and thus must be losing money
on each cup of coffee they sell.

As we're all in this together, I've decided to help

them stop losing money, by giving up buying coffee from them. If enough of us do it, they will soon return to profitability.

Griff Griffith
London E11

SIR – Rather than boycott Starbucks why not order coffee, sit at a table and stay for as many hours as you like? You are undoubtedly behaving badly but are not doing anything illegal.

Dick Laurence
Wells, Somerset

SIR – Perhaps the country would be better served if the financial directors of Starbucks, Amazon and Google managed its financial affairs.

Bob Cole
Newton Tony, Wiltshire

NEW MAN FOR THE OLD LADY

SIR – My friend's future daughter-in-law, an experienced, English-speaking A&E nurse from Toronto, arrived in the UK two weeks ago. She has had to pay $300 to sit an English test before she can apply for a job here.

Has our prospective Governor of the Bank of England been required to do the same?

S.R.
Edinburgh

SIR – There may have been rumblings about the new Governor of the Bank of England being a foreigner – but at least he's not an Old Etonian.

Elizabeth Gillow
Stone, Staffordshire

SIR – Mark Carney is not a foreigner. François Hollande and Angela Merkel are foreigners. Herman van Rompuy and José Manuel Barroso are foreigners. Mark Carney is one of us, or as near as makes no difference.

I will be voting Ukip, by the way.

Michael Phillips
Bexhill-on-Sea, East Sussex

UKIP'S RUDE AWAKENING

SIR – What a gift for a Conference speech writer: 'Ukip if you want to . . .'.

Robert Stephenson
Henley-on-Thames, Oxfordshire

SIR — The person who called me and others 'swivel-eyed loons' is obviously unaware that a *loon* is another name for the very handsome Great Northern Diver, a far-sighted bird that breeds in the far north of Canada but migrates to our shores for the winter.

Jeremy Brittain-Long
Constantine, Cornwall

SIR — Swivel-eyed people have the advantage of being able to see the big picture. Perhaps we need a few more swivel eyes in Downing Street and Whitehall.

Alistair Macdonald
Eastbourne, East Sussex

SIR — Anyone for the Swivel-eyed Loon Party? The public hasn't had much fun in politics since Screaming Lord Such departed.

Derek Sharp
Torquay, Devon

SIR — The language of the Lower Fourth seems to prevail these days: *swivel-eyed loons*, *fruitcakes*, *clowns*, *plebs*. At least John Major used medieval Latin to refer to some members of the party as *bastards*.

Linda Read
London SW14

SIR — My husband considers himself to have
what are now described as 'traditional' Tory views
on many subjects. Recently he has made mention of
joining Ukip. Does our family name mean he will
automatically be destined for high office in
that party?

Jackie Circus
Holton, Suffolk

SIR — David Cameron should be careful using
bakery analogies. Fruitcake has a very long shelf-life,
though that of yesterday's crumpet is very short.

Tim Spencer
Bexhill-on-Sea, East Sussex

SIR — Evidently a quarter of the electorate like
fruitcake.

Stuart G. Bevan
Newbury, Berkshire

SIR — Your columns have referred to 'Loongate' and
'Swivelgate'. Perhaps there should be a referendum
to determine which of these passes into history.

Geoffrey White
Wellow, Somerset

SIR – You seem to have become a great supporter of Nigel Farage. The Malay word for vagina is *faraj*, pronounced *farage*. As he is full of wind, he could have two rude nicknames.

John Evans
Buxted, East Sussex

FATHER BALLS

SIR – The photograph of Ed Balls dressed up as Father Christmas made me rather wistful. Why can't we just see Mr Balls at Christmas?

Juliet Henderson
South Warnborough, Hampshire

SIR – The gangly, slightly awkward sixth-form prefect and the red-faced, overweight, aggressive year-eleven pupil would make an interesting scenario in an education setting but it is no way to run an opposition party in Westminster. As long as Mr Miliband and Mr Balls dominate the Labour party David Cameron and his colleagues can continue to make their errors in peace.

Mick Ferrie
Mawnan Smith, Cornwall

JOBS FOR THE (OLD) BOYS

SIR — Your correspondent says that Ed Miliband's call for MPs to 'quit second jobs could lead to an exodus of those with real world business experience'. For many years I have dreamed of us being governed by 100 people: 60 business people, 20 from the judiciary and 20 intelligent people over 70 years of age.

I am 90, but I could be one of them as I know exactly all the drastic action that is needed in this country.

Tom Tooley
Hambleton, Lancashire

SIR — Surely the reason Ed Miliband is against MPs having a second job is that most Labour MPs are unemployable?

Brian Christley
Abergele, Conwy

SIR — Can I request that IPSA sets the level for my state pension in future?

Philip Howells
Worsley, Manchester

BARRY THOMAS RESPONDS TO BRIAN LEVESON

SIR – I have just read on the banner at the bottom of the BBC News channel screen that someone called JK Rowling is dismayed at the Prime Minister's response to the Leveson Report. May I through your columns let it be known that Barry Thomas is heartened by the Prime Minister's response?

Barry Thomas
Thurston, Suffolk

SIR – Put it this way, if Nick Clegg, Ed Miliband and Gerry McCann all agree a certain action is correct, it can't be.

David Andrews
Bacup, Lancashire

SIR – Most rational people would happily accept a law that prohibited newspapers from mentioning, in any context, Hugh Grant, Steve Coogan and Charlotte Church.

Michael Stanford
London SE23

SIR — Yesterday I read aloud an article from the Travel section of the *Telegraph* to my wife, who was googling on her iPad. The piece mentioned Camps Bay, South Africa, and as we had stayed there in March, we had a brief conversation about it.

Scarcely had we finished when up popped an advertisement on her screen for accommodation at Camps Bay. This could surely not have been coincidence as my wife had not entered the name on any search engine. Rather, it was a Leveson moment, as the computer had 'heard' us.

It used to be said that one should mind what one said before children and servants. Now that would appear to include one's computer as well.

Robert Sunderland
Little Wymondley, Hertfordshire

PLANNING PICKLES

SIR — Eric Pickles, who seems so keen on planning reform, should appreciate the problems faced when an ever-expanding waistline meets a maximum available trouser size. You either limit your consumption or you ruin your trousers.

Substitute countryside and environment for trousers, Mr Pickles, and you should start to get the picture.

Gary F.S. Knight
Colchester, Essex

SIR — MPs are saying that we should eat less meat. Judging by the not uncommon sight of bulging blouses and protruding paunches in the House of Commons, might I suggest that some of them just try eating a bit less.

Ted Shorter
Hildenborough, Kent

SIR — You report that Ed Balls has been fined for jumping a red light. Are you sure it wasn't Yvette Cooper who was driving?

W.K. Wood
Bolton, Lancashire

THE PRYCE OF HUHNE'S HUBRIS

SIR — Perhaps Chris Huhne should now change his personalised registration plate from H11 HNE to HUBR 1 S.

Nigel Dyson
Ashley, Hampshire

SIR — Vicky Pryce's revenge on Chris Huhne makes a change from cutting his best suits to shreds with scissors and throwing his prized wines into the street.

J. Driver
Bentley, Hampshire

SIR — The kindest comment one can make about Mr Huhne is that he would not be a very good bridge player.

Mike Edwards
Haslemere, Surrey

SIR — My husband is pressuring me to take his Nectar points so that he can have my Avios points. What is a wife to do?

Diane B. Choyce
London W2

SIR — It's a shame a more creative punishment could not have been devised. Forcing the two miscreants to have sole occupancy of a *Big Brother* room for a week would have represented a splendid outcome, both in terms of humiliation and public voyeurism, not to mention the producers' profits on such a venture, which could have been given to a suitable charity.

Tim Maddox
London N1

SIR — Here's a neat way to tie up two contemporary loose ends: let's have a state funeral for Richard III and bury Chris Huhne in the parking lot.

Malcolm Clark
Welwyn, Hertfordshire

SIR — If Richard III has set a precedent, we should hear of the whereabouts of Gordon Brown in the year 2539.

Brian Christley
Abergele, Conwy

SIR — I am in the hitherto unlikely position of feeling a little sorry for Nick Clegg. Saddled with David Laws, Vince Cable and Simon Hughes, not to mention ex-colleagues of painful memory such as Mark Oaten, Charles Kennedy, Lembit Opik and Chris Huhne, he must wonder whether he did something wrong in a previous life.

Tim Hubbard
London SW14

SIR — Do the Liberal Democrats wear sandals because they are easy to kick off in sexual emergencies?

Dr Alan D. Prowse
Leatherhead, Surrey

SIR – This coalition Government looks increasingly like a teabag full of wet dregs.

Richard Shaw
Dunstable, Bedfordshire

SIR – Eric Linklater created the character of Magnus Merriman MP, a politician whose best laid plans always went astray. The author wrote of him, 'If he went a-courting in my lady's chamber, he would trip over the pot.'

This Government reminds me of Magnus Merriman.

Dennis Callaghan
Liverpool

NUL POINTS FOR THE TORIES

SIR – Ironically, since 1997, the fate of the Conservatives has mirrored that of the United Kingdom at the Eurovision Song Contest. On May 1 1997, the Conservative Party lost its last working majority to Labour and two days later, the United Kingdom won its last Eurovision Song Contest.

In the intervening 16 years, neither the UK nor the Conservatives have selected a winner capable of winning the hearts of the voters.

There may yet be hope for both. David Cameron could formulate a new vision for Europe and Ann Widdecombe may yet consider a career in pop music.

Anthony Rodriguez
Staines-upon-Thames, Middlesex

RIP MARMITE THATCHER

SIR – Having seen the vast amount of varying comments about Margaret Thatcher it appears to me that perhaps she should now be known as Marmite Thatcher.

Chris Shore
East Preston, West Sussex

SIR – I'll say one thing for Margaret Thatcher: unlike Blair or Cameron, she could always be relied upon to stab you in the front.

Mike Wright
Nuneaton, Warwickshire

SIR – I am bitterly disappointed; I had presumed that she was immortal.

Charles Holcombe
Brighton

SIR — Please can we have a break from articles about Mrs Thatcher. Kim Jong-il will begin to think that this country was ruled by a cult of personality.

B.N. Bosworth
Blakedown, Worcestershire

SIR — Crossword buffs among your readers will undoubtedly know that '*The Daily Telegraph*' is an anagram for 'I help the great lady'. This was pointed out in a letter to the *Guardian* on October 29 1982

John Adamson
Cambridge

SIR — I would like to register my extreme pleasure at the degree of Schadenfraude in evidence following the death of your High Priestess. I revel in your frustration. I relish your ire. I bathe in the tears of her supporters and ideological offspring. Two dozen plagues on all of you.

Anon

SIR — I wonder what the result would be of comparing the average IQ of those people who denigrate Mrs Thatcher's memory with the average IQ of those who celebrate her life.

Ronald E. Pitt
Fishguard, Pembrokeshire

SIR – Does not the argument about the 'Ding Dong' song merely prove that a few of the troublemakers, of whom Mrs Thatcher tried to rid us, still exist?

The Government clearly has more work to do.

Brian Vaughton
Whitford, Devon

SIR – Baroness Thatcher was the most courageous woman this country has seen since Elizabeth I. Is it too late to make 'Rule Britannia' top of the charts?

S.T.
Golden Green, Kent

SIR – Interviewed on Al Jazeera, a protester first blamed Baroness Thatcher for closing the mines, which is debatable, and then claimed that if the Tories had their way, 14-year-old children would still be going down the mines.

John G. Prescott
Coulsdon, Surrey

SIR – In the 1970s, in a small village market in Yugoslavia, the local lad running the vegetable stall was bemoaning in broken English the fact that they had rampant inflation.

I said to him: 'What you need is Margaret Thatcher.'

Quick as a flash, he said: 'No, what I need is Samantha Fox.'

Carole Buchanan
Wadebridge, Cornwall

SIR — Hearing of the sad death of Lady Thatcher reminded me that, for many years, my wife displayed on her desk at work a cutting from your newspaper: 'Behind every great woman is a Denis'.

Denis Graves
Crowborough, East Sussex

SIR — In all the analysis of Lady Thatcher's political and personal attributes, I feel that one important item has been overlooked: her Christian name.

I have never met a Margaret who did not know who she was, where she was, where she was going and what she was going to do when she got there.

Capt Kim Mockett (husband of Mrs Margaret Mockett)
Littlebourne, Kent

SIR — Lady Thatcher's funeral service began with a quotation from TS Eliot's *Four Quartets*. Perhaps an extract from *The Wasteland* would have been more appropriate.

> **P.D.J. MacGregor**
> Nickley Wood, Kent

SIR – Having personally faced vitriolic responses to Margaret Thatcher's legacy, I now know how St Peter felt.

> **Michael Cattell**
> Mollington, Cheshire

SIR – Amid all the controversy, I think I can hear a clear, forceful voice: 'I'm enjoying this!'

> **I.P.F. Meiklejohn**
> Forres, Moray

SIR – Wherever she is, the implosion of the EU will be amusing her.

> **V.G.**
> Tokyo

BELGIUM WAFFLES

SIR — May I please add to the laurels of your excellent political department by leaking a copy of the Prime Minister's speech on Europe?

It will run as follows: 'Blah, blah, waffle, waffle . . . influence in the corridors of power . . . lunching [sic] above our weight . . . stranded in mid Atlantic . . . I know better than the British people, which is why I am determined not to allow them to express their opinion . . . the political class does very well out of Brussels . . . you proles can stuff it . . . blah, blah, waffle, waffle.'

Peter Croft
Cambridge

SIR — You report that Ed Miliband is concerned that David Cameron may be sleepwalking towards the EU exit. Much of the UK would like him to wake up and break into a brisk run.

Ian Brown
Derby

SIR – I see in your Cyprus Bailout Live blog, at 13.55, a reference to the 'Finish [sic] Europe Minister'. Thank goodness it is all over.

Brian Gilbert
Hampton, Middlesex

SIR – Yesterday my friend visited Bath and promised to bring me a Bath bun for my tea. At a supermarket bakery counter she was offered Belgian buns instead. Is this because of another EU directive?

Derek Gregory
Castle Cary, Somerset

SIR – Am I alone in thinking that the EU's statement that minimum alcohol pricing would be illegal is the first time in all these years it has done something sensible?

Fred Rawson
Reigate, Surrey

SIR – Would it be more acceptable to the City of London if the European Commission were to place a bowler hat on bankers bonuses, rather than a cap?

Richard Tyson-Davies
Newdigate, Surrey

SIR — At my golf club there are different categories of membership, including a discounted country membership for those who live at some distance from the club.

I am sure the United Kingdom is far enough away from Brussels to qualify.

Harry Stevens
Upper Bentley, Worcestershire

SIR — Browsing the letters page today I notice that all the letters about *Les Misérables* are written by women and all the letters written about the EU referendum are from men. Was this deliberate?

Ruth Cliff
Uckfield, East Sussex

SIR — Before we renegotiate the terms of our membership with Europe, which might end the free movement of labour, might I remind Prince Charles that a post has become available in Holland?

Richard Hodder
Four Elms, Kent

DUKES, DUCHESSES AND DUNCES

THE ROYAL TELEGRAPH

SIR – Am I alone in noticing that the Queen looks far happier on the front page of the *Telegraph* than in the *Guardian*? Is she trying to tell us something?

Fred Ford
Salford

HIGH-VISIBILITY HARRY

SIR – Your photograph of Prince Harry at the Chelsea Flower Show in a dayglow yellow waistcoat prompted me to think that he is one of a select few in this country who have absolutely no need of such a garment. In fact, he would probably pay good money if someone could come up with its opposite: a low-vis jacket.

Sam Kelly
Dobcross, Oldham

SIR – What a coup for the *Telegraph*. For two days running now, you have published pictures of Prince Harry with his trousers on.

Clive Pilley
Westcliff-on-Sea, Essex

SIR – It must have been quite a shock for Prince Harry on his second visit to America this year to see so many American women with their clothes on.

Brian Christley
Abergele, Conwy

SIR – Prince Harry's statement, 'If there's people trying to do bad stuff to our guys then we'll take them out of the game' suggests we should increase the level of security David Cameron and George Osborne receive if they go ahead with the Armed Forces redundancy programme.

D.W.
Market Lavington, Wiltshire

MANTEL VS. MIDDLETON

SIR – Consider Hilary Mantel's description of the Duchess as a 'shop window mannequin' versus *The Daily Telegraph*'s description of 'The Duchess, whose pregnancy bump was visible for the first time in public through her flimsy Max Mara dress . . .'
1-0 to Hilary Mantel, I would suggest.

Andrew Stewart
Reigate, Surrey

SIR — Thank you for using your front page headline, 'Duchess with baby on board' to provide such a perfect illustration of Hilary Mantel's thesis.

Barbara Burfoot
Alton, Hampshire

SIR — She was just too kind. The word is *bimbo*.

P.P.
Truro, Cornwall

SIR — Mannequin princess? That's rich coming from a tubby in a tent.

Joseph G. Dawson
Withnell, Cheshire

SIR — Look, you do not need to be particularly observant to note that 99 per cent of writers, whether they be novelists, historians or whatever, are not particularly nice human beings. I cannot think of a single columnist I would want within a million miles of my fondly imagined South Sea Island paradise.

Huw Beynon
Llandeilo, Carmarthenshire

TREASONABLE ROYAL PORTRAITS

SIR — Had the artist Dan Llywelyn Hall produced such a ghastly image for Elizabeth I, he'd be in the Tower waiting to have his head struck off.

Robert Readman
Bournemouth, Dorset

SIR — I wonder what the Duchess of Cambridge would have looked like had she been painted by Modigliani.

Duncan Rayner
Sunningdale, Berkshire

SIR — Congratulations to Paul Emsley for his wonderful portrait of Jennifer Aniston.

Jeff Tonge
Bolton

ROYAL BABY BLUES

SIR — I am very pro-Royal, but after today's announcement of the Duchess of Cambridge's pregnancy, will somebody please hurry up and

implement the Leveson Report and save us all
from the interminable speculation?

Gordon Bain
Ditchling, East Sussex

SIR — How prescient of Boris Johnson, who in early
September praised Great Britain's Olympic athletes
with the words, 'You not only inspired a generation,
but you probably helped to create one as well.'

Jolly well done, Boris. But how could you have
known?

Paul Harrison
Terling, Essex

SIR — I read that the Duchess of Cambridge is
considering whether to give birth at the Royal
Berkshire Hospital. I feel that my experience there
may help her to decide.

Some years ago, while recovering from brain
surgery, I was placed in a mixed ward. One afternoon
the peace was shattered by a naked young man who
ran the length of the ward, hotly pursued by nurses.

In an effort to evade capture he jumped into bed
with me and attempted to pull the covers over us.
He was eventually sedated and removed.

I would urge her Royal Highness to insist on a
private room.

Eileen Letestu
Geneva, Switzerland

SIR — I hope those two colonial plate spinners who played a prank call on the hospital are pleased with themselves. Someone should point out to them that life is not a lager advert. If they were not already in a penal colony that is where they should be sent.

T. I. Sanderson
Nuneaton, Warwickshire

SIR — I boiled four eggs yesterday. When I cut them all had double yolks. Is this a sign?

Anne Peebles
Pentyrch, Cardiff

SIR — Napoleonic law deemed that the second born inherited the title, under the wonderfully Gallic logic that the second one 'out' must have been the first one 'put in'.

P. Weston-Davies
South Scarle, Nottinghamshire

SIR — Shouldn't the future monarch be decided by the flick of a coin — obviously half a crown?

Charles and Alison Lewis
Taffs Well, Cardiff

SIR — If there is to be another six months of this stuff I shall be joining poor Kate in hospital with uncontrollable nausea.

Alison Place
Hampton, Middlesex

SIR — In my day we just had children without the need for publicity or, indeed, being taken to hospital for morning sickness. Is this now fashionable?

I went to Singapore with my son aged four months in a sky cradle. He is now 43 with two daughters.

Backbone, William and Kate, backbone.

Judith Scott
St Ives, Cambridgeshire

SIR — Can someone tell Bryony Gordon that she and the Duchess of Cambridge are not the only women who are pregnant, however special they must feel.

Jeremy Gibbons QC
Mannington, Dorset

SIR — Two days of news about the Duchess of Cambridge, and you haven't yet told us about her hospital gown. Who designed it? How much did it cost? And has she worn it before?

J.S. Hillmore
London N20

SIR – Your front-page headline, 'I'm not excited by royal baby, says Queen's cousin' must rank among the most boring ever.

Readers may care to know that I am not excited by the possibility of Wayne Rooney being transferred from Manchester United.

Leonard Macauley
Staining, Lancashire

SIR – How fortunate that the Royal birth did not occur during Sunday's Ashes Test finale. As a young schoolboy in August 1950, I was present at the Oval for the fourth Test between England and West Indies when play was stopped to announce the birth of Princess Anne.

I recall that it did not go down well. Cricket, it would appear, reigns supreme.

Let's hope something turns up before Thursday.

James Algar
Hockley, Essex

SIR – Maybe the hospital could release pink or blue smoke when the baby is born.

Michael Robinson
Chillert, Isle of Wight

SIR – Surely the Royal baby cannot be allowed to arrive when Matt is on holiday?

Alan Mooge
Enfield, Middlesex

SIR – Please can we have an 'anti-wittering' button added to the BBC.

Harry Nightingale
West Byfleet, Surrey

SIR – Never in the history of news reporting, have so few facts been stretched so far, for so long, by so many.

Roger Castle
Cardiff

SIR – How civilised to announce the birth between *University Challenge* and *Rick Stein's India*, and while Nicholas Witchell had gone off air.

M.C.
Chilworth, Surrey

SIR — With the arrival of our future king, can we expect his aunt to write a book on how to bring up a baby and party at the same time?

John R. Corsan
Ashcott, Somerset

SIR — I can't wait to hear what Helen Mirren has to say on the Royal birth.

Valda Mossman
Penzance, Cornwall

SIR — A name for the new prince? In keeping with modern Britain, how about Jordan, Jayden or Connor?

Clifford Baxter
Wareham, Dorset

SIR — I think the baby should be named Finn. He could then be known as Buckleberry Finn.

Robert Smith
Worcester

SIR — Why not call him Austin?

Mike Brett
London N13

SIR — With the joy of fatherhood Prince William seems to have completely forgotten to pronounce his Hs. Perhaps the Royal baby will be known as 'Enry.

Ben Davies
Oxshott, Surrey

SIR — Not many people know this, but the Duchess of Cambridge's pet name for her husband is Dukey, pronounced *Duckie*. And he and Harry collect teddy bears.

V.L.
Shepperton, Middlesex

SIR — We might now have the interesting sequence of Elizabeth II, Charles III, William V and George VII, thus involving the first four prime numbers.

K. B-C.
Maidstone, Kent

SIR — I have just seen our future King apologise to the waiting journalists for his son's tardiness saying, 'I know how long you've all been sat out here . . .'

Were my wife and I the only ones shouting at the screen, 'Sitting'?

Chris Harding
Finchfield, West Midlands

THE USE AND ABUSE OF LANGUAGE

THE FUTURE OF ENGLISH

SIR — Hats off to head teacher Carol Walker for her attempts to encourage standard English.

During a recent visit to a supermarket in Darlington I overheard the following exchange between a small boy and his father in the sweetie aisle.

Small boy (pointing): 'I want them ones.'

Father: 'No, it's, "I want them ones, please".'

It's going to be a long struggle.

Brian Jones
Darlington, County Durham

SIR — When my husband was in hospital and very ill, he remarked: 'If only there was some respite.' The nurse glared at him and replied: 'We respect everyone in this hospital.'

He decided it was better to say nothing.

Margaret Gilbertson
Atherton, Lancashire

SIR — Several days ago, I visited a younger relative, who is the mother of three children. She told me about their after-school activities: 'On Mondays, it's like drama and swimming. On Tuesdays, it's like Cubs and music. On Wednesday, it's like cricket and tennis. On Thursday, it's like a night off, and we are like, phew. On Fridays, it's like Scouts. On Saturdays, we're like ready for a rest.'

Did I miss something? What is wrong with, like, old-fashioned grammar?

Sarah Carmichael Wallace
Moffat, Dumfriesshire

SIR — The dinner lady at my granddaughter's primary school accompanies dishing out baked beans with: 'The more you eat, the more you fart.'

A.B.
Donhead St Andrew, Wiltshire

SIR — When as a child I politely asked my teacher what she had written in red ink by my work it turned out to be 'Your writing is illegible.'

Mrs J. Rogerson
Ramsbury, Wiltshire

THE BEGINNING OF THE END

SIR — Am I alone in being alarmed by the health-food fad creeping into the Scriptures? *Alpha* and *Omega* were read in my local church over Easter as *Alpha* and *Omeeega*.

The introduction of polyunsaturated fatty acids into sermons is a distracting novelty.

Robert Hood-Wright
Nanstallon, Cornwall

INTRODUCING THE INTERNET

SIR – For 'www' I must admit that I usually say 'Weeweewee'. It's quick, it's easy, it's not been misunderstood yet and it always raises a smile.

Kenneth Rainey
Goring-by-Sea, West Sussex

SIR – Wee Willie Winkie – more syllables, but quicker.

Anthony F. Bainbridge
Codford, Wiltshire

SIR – My mother calls it 'that www dot thing' – apt rather than easy.

Kate Graeme-Cook
Tarrant Launceston, Dorset

SIR – How about abbreviating www to worldwide web?

Rev. Roger Holmes
York

A FLUSH OF LINGUISTIC
CONUNDRUMS

SIR — Mandrake reports that four prominent
jailbirds were seen at the theatre. I am unable to
discover the collective noun for jailbirds. A *flush* or a
flight, perhaps?

> **Tim Deane**
> Tisbury, Wiltshire

SIR — Christine Odone describes Jeffrey Archer as
'uxorious'. Is there a similar word for a wife who is
excessively fond of her husband?

Similarly, is there a female equivalent of *misogynist*,
to describe a woman who hates men?

> **Les Sharp**
> Hersham, Surrey

SIR — Your letter-writer is incorrect. Criminals
are not the only ones to be described in non-
sexist language. My grandson was delivered by a
gentleman, who was introduced as a 'midwife',
rather than as a 'midperson'.

> **Leslie Meynell**
> Stockton-on-Tees, County Durham

SIR — Why is a female teacher described as
'romantically pursuing' a pupil, when a male teacher
would be 'grooming' a pupil?

Peter Iden
Totnes, Devon

SIR — When an injured jockey is described as being
'in a stable condition', what is the equine equivalent?

Jeremy Nicholas
Great Bardfield, Essex

SIR — Can anyone tell me who invented the term
'the gravy train'? Better still, can anyone tell me how
to get a ticket?

Ginny Batchelor-Smith
Lower Assenden, Oxfordshire

SIR — I rang to book a restaurant on Monday, saying
I would like a table for next Sunday. I was then asked
whether I wanted this Sunday or next Sunday, to
which I replied I wanted the Sunday in six days' time.
  How did this confusion arise? Why would
'next Sunday' mean the next Sunday after the
next Sunday?

Michael Fleming
Cobham, Surrey

THE JOY OF FRACKING

SIR – The word *fracking* demonstrates the superiority of our glorious language. In France, L'Académie française would take several years to decide upon a suitably Romano-Gallic word, while in Germany a Technische Amt might produce a quicker result, but it would fill half a column of this newspaper.

Tony Pay
Bridge of Cally, Perthshire

SIR – I have always wondered about the word *futtocks*, but to my joy, these wooden brackets can clearly be seen in action in your excellent photograph of the interior of the *Mary Rose*. Well worth the 30-year wait.

Roy Selwyn
Selborne, Hampshire

CLEARER SWEARING, PLEASE

SIR – Thinking about going to see *The Book of Mormon*? Worried about the amount of bad language in the show? Don't be. Despite the good acoustics and excellent sound system of the Prince of Wales

Theatre, the diction of the cast is so poor that you won't hear much that upsets you.

I suspect that I am not typical of many *Telegraph* readers in that I can put up with any amount of profanity on the stage, if the show is good. From my seat in the third row of the stalls I heard not a single 'c' word all evening.

I felt a bit short-changed, actually.

Andrew Luff
London NW1

SIR — My wife's new year's resolution — not to swear at our large boisterous black Labrador — was broken within four seconds of midnight when he launched himself at us while we were dancing to *Auld Lang Syne*.

Is this a record for brevity?

Hugh Bebb
Sunbury-on-Thames, Middlesex

SIR — My new year's resolution is not to send you any more letters.

Brian Wilkinson
Garmouth, Moray

THE LANGUAGE POLICE

SIR — Andrew Mitchell, the former Chief Whip, is said to have called a policeman a 'f****** pleb'. Last year John Terry, the Chelsea and England footballer, allegedly called Anton Ferdinand, another footballer, a 'f****** black ****'.

Neither recipient of the abuse apparently objected to the profanities but were offended by the words *pleb* and *black*. What is this country coming to?

Bruce Denness
Whitwell, Isle of Wight

SIR — As a life-long Classics master now well stricken in years, what amazes me most about the never-ending plebgate row is the contrast between my own gently disintegrating frame and the astonishing vigour of the Latin language, which retains undimmed the power to shock and outrage with a single word. *Cruda viridisque senectus* indeed!

John Holland
Bedford

SIR — If the former Government Chief Whip had used the classical Greek term *hoi polloi* instead of *pleb* he might have kept his job. Most dogberries would have assumed he was talking about a high-street fashion store – but only if he had put the stress on the wrong syllable.

Yours filthily,
David McA. McKirdy
Mansfield Woodhouse, Nottinghamshire

SIR – In the past few weeks the *Telegraph* – and even the *Radio Times* – have published articles indicating the use of swear words by means of asterisks. Why should readers be beset by this habit? The asterisks hide nothing.

Maybe the Government should step in.

Michael Burton
Easton, Somerset

SIR – Last night's BBC News showed policemen wearing T-shirts bearing the message 'PC Pleb and proud'. If so, what are they upset about?

Andrew Allen
Mobberley, Cheshire

SIR – The notoriously imaginative subtitling service of the BBC's news bulletin today excelled itself. As the subtitle told the hard-of-hearing twice: 'He [Andrew Mitchell] denied calling the officer a Clegg and a moron.'

Robin Stafford
Goudhurst, Kent

SIR – Your Women's Editor, Emma Barnett, was on
Sky News this morning. According to the subtitles, she
was saying that the late Prime Minister was 'stabbed in
the back by the Old Italians in her cabinet'.

Stephen Hargrave
London WC1

THE MEDIA VS. THE ENGLISH LANGUAGE

SIR – I have just watched the BBC's *One O'Clock
News* and cannot believe what they are doing to
the English language. Why is it the 'thing' now to
change Ws to Rs, thus creating a whole new lexicon
of meaningless words?

Law has been changed to *lorr*, *drawing* to *drorring*,
saw to *sorr*.

The W has gone missing from the whole
of television and radio and I, for one, want it
back, please.

Richard Davies
Heath Charnock, Lancashire

SIR – Can I recommend your readers watch the Tour de France on television. It is so exciting and as a bonus, you can hear the word *kilometre* pronounced correctly.

Kevin Murnan
Bridgend, South Wales

SIR – I have been listening to the BBC News the last few days and have heard them constantly referring to the 'sex industry' and 'sex workers'. Does the BBC have a policy that forbids the use of *prostitution* and *prostitutes*?

Alan Self
Crowborough, East Sussex

SIR – I have some sympathy with your correspondent's frustration with ITV presenters and their 'Welcome back' after a commercial break.

During my years as an ITN newscaster I would begin with, 'Good evening' and then proceed to report how dreadful it was.

Michael Nicholson
Grayswood, Surrey

SIR – Listening earlier today to coverage of the Algerian crisis the BBC anchorman asked the correspondent to 'tell us what we know'. Please, I tuned in to find out some news.

Mark Wade
Woodley, Berkshire

TOO MUCH WEATHER

SIR – This morning I heard a weather forecaster on the radio inform us that we were 'going to have a lot of weather'.

Sally Jaspars
Aberdeen

SIR – Every form of weather – rain, snow, ice, wind and flood – now has to be qualified as an 'event'.

Charles Foster
Chalfont St Peter, Buckinghamshire

SIR – Now that the floods are thankfully receding, might we have some respite from the use of the word *respite* by the weather forecasters?

Lucette Rees
Calne, Wiltshire

PAINFULLY POOR REPORTING

SIR — Sadly, the falling standards of writing at the *Telegraph* are in step with the general decline now axiomatic of modern life. I am learning to adapt to a quality of grammar which would have warranted considerable pain from the corporal punishment of my school days, but this morning's headline, 'Fathers get to share new mother's year of parental leave' has proved beyond my ability to keep pace with these changes.

You may be reluctant to disturb the integrity of the copy submitted by your correspondent but you most certainly should have jumped on the person responsible for this execrable headline. Why are multiple fathers seemingly to share a year of parental leave with only one woman? Or should I say 'get to share...'?

This is disgraceful and should invite the censure of that splendid Mr Gove.

Dermot Elworthy
Tiverton, Devon

SIR — Nothing upsets me more than the ubiquitous wrongly attached phrase or participle. I frequently receive letters beginning, 'As a valued customer, I am writing to tell you about . . .', where the writer has turned himself into the customer.

I don't expect to find such nonsense in the *Telegraph*, but it would appear that even the best journalists are not immune. According to the account on page three of the Duchess of Cambridge's visit to Cambridge, the wind in Cambridge has a darker, heavy-parted fringe. I am still trying to picture this.

Jill Lamley
Hampson, Lancashire

SIR – I am confident that the Pope's brother is able to speak grammatically, so it is sad that in translation you write 'it is simply the case that people didn't used to become as old'.

This is the second time this week that I have noticed this ugly solecism in your pages. The *Telegraph* should and could do better.

Elizabeth Morland
Stanford in the Vale, Oxfordshire

SIR – I was amused to read that the two Russians who discovered the wreckage of a light aircraft were out 'grouse hunting', an expression unfamiliar to the shooting fraternity in this country.

Sandy Pratt
Lingfield, Surrey

SIR — Since your correspondent is content to describe himself as a *chair*, it seems he has difficulty counting the number of legs he possesses. This being so, I am surprised he should be considered capable of criticising private schools, or indeed anyone else.

Roger Merryweather
Whiteshill, Gloucestershire

SIR — You describe my colleague Professor Norman Williams PRCS as a 'top doctor'. As his area of expertise is the colorectum, this would appear to transgress the Trades Description Act.

Douglas Bamford
Combe Down, Somerset

NOTHING TO SEE HERE

SIR — Your article on blue plaques reminded me of the one my wife and I saw in Ludlow. It read simply, 'No one of any particular significance ever lived here.'

Philip Watts
Sutton Coldfield, West Midlands

SIR – My favourite sign in Swindon: 'No fly tipping offenders will be prosecuted.'

Moira Brodie
Bourton, Wiltshire

SIR – I was amused to read the following in the local *Methodist Magazine*: 'Eight new choir robes are currently needed due to the addition of several new members and the deterioration of some older ones.'

G.B. Tolcher
Budleigh Salterton, Devon

WORRYINGLY PREDICTIVE TEXT MESSAGES

SIR – My neighbour sent me a text to apologise for her dogs barking noisily. I replied: 'No problem, we are both old and deaf.'

This read: 'No problem, we are both old and dead.'

In our opinion this is carrying predictive text too far.

Catriona Craig
Clevelode, Worcestershire

SIR — Predictive text messages turn my brother Stan, who is a really nice man, into Satan.

Henry Maj
Armitage, Staffordshire

SIR — Last year my wife and I went away for a weekend in Bristol. In her daily text to our daughter my wife sent: 'Took him to see the *Great Britain*'.

Unfortunately predictive text translated 'him' as 'Igor', which led to some interesting questions about who she was actually spending her weekend with, and did I know?

Andy Ritchie
Loxwood, West Sussex

SIR — I recall the pleasure of trying out my letter-writing skill on my new desktop computer. When I typed my forename, imagine my shock to receive the message, 'Rodney — word not recognised, try Rodent.'

Am I the only person to be insulted by an inanimate object?

Rodney Stone
Burbage, Wiltshire

SIR — According to my spell checker I used to be Wanton before I got married.

Phillipa Tootill (née Swanton)
Otley, West Yorkshire

SIR — A while ago I wrote a letter to a friend in Ogmore-by-Sea, South Wales. When I used the spell check, it was suggested I change 'Ogmore' for 'Gomorra'.

Since then I have often wondered what my computer knew about Ogmore that I did not.

Pete Griffiths
Grays, Essex

'OO TER SPEK THE KING'S ENGLISH

SIR — For years the Brummie accent has been a source of mockery, even scorn, but now, thanks to research by the University of Leicester, it seems that Richard III may have spoken in this region's vernacular.

When we open our mouths and folk try to hide a smile, we can now hold our heads high in the knowledge that we speak the King's English.

Barry Jones
Ryde, Isle of Wight

SIR — Some years ago I flew to Los Angeles on a business trip and went to the car rental desk to arrange to collect a car. The young lady behind the desk was obviously intrigued by my accent (middle England) and looking at my driving licence, asked if I came from the United Kingdom.

When I said yes she asked, 'And do they speak English there?'

Brian Raybould
Portishead, Somerset

SIR — When my husband, with his broad Yorkshire accent, first became a college fellow over 40 years ago, an elderly academic asked him patronisingly, 'And are you having problems with the accent?'

'No,' he replied. 'If you speak slowly I can understand most of what you say.'

Jean Robinson
Oxford

I'M BAD

SIR — On being introduced to a man I had never met before, I said, 'Hello, how are you?' 'I'm good,' was his reply.

'And who told you that?'

Bad girl. I know it was very rude of me and he was rather taken aback, especially at the guffaws from others present. I just couldn't stop myself.

I did apologise immediately, I hasten to add. But really!

Pauline Turner
Knutsford, Cheshire

SIR – I have the misfortune of working with a young man who prefers to conclude telephone conversations urging me to, 'Keep it real, man.'

I'm sure this is good advice if only I knew what 'it' refers to. Once I find out I will assure him that I will do everything possible to prevent it falling into the hands of the imaginary.

Andrew Woodward
Luak Bay, Malaysia

JTJ (JARGON THAT JARRS)

SIR – Recently I was asked my opinion on a colleague's report. I said that I had found it hard to understand, because it contained so many TLAs. To my gratification, I was then asked what a TLA was.

Simon Crewe
Plymouth

SIR — It seems from your report that 'efficiency savings' in the public sector have nudged me out of my 'comfort zone' into a 'stretch zone'. From this challenging new position my colleagues and I shall deliver 'reablement' to our patients.

Dr R. Chesterman
Braintree, Essex

EVERY LITTLE HURTS

SIR — Tesco's attempt at alliteration on its luxury loo rolls — 'same luxury less lorries' - might be a nice labelling ploy, but it is cause to wince. Is the word *fewer* beyond the intelligence of the average Tesco shopper? Or, more likely, is there an ignoramus in marketing who thinks taking liberties with grammar is cool?

C.F.
Chalfont St Peter, Buckinghamshire

SIR — Tesco's delivery vans display pictures of tomatoes and asparagus alongside the words 'freshly clicked'. Is any phrase more likely to divorce consumers from the true source of their food?

Andrew Blake
Shalbourne, Wiltshire

SIR – The latest example of sloppy language seen in shops is, 'We do not currently range this accessory in store.'

Sandy Pratt
Lingfield, Surrey

SIR – One of the most puzzling and nonsensical expressions used by shop assistants is, 'There you go'. I am tempted to ask, 'Where do I go and what do I do when I get there?'

R.E. Jones
West Horsley, Surrey

SIR – Since when did, 'Are you alright there?' come to mean, 'Can I help you?'

Andrew Tooby
Ombersley, Worcestershire

SIR – It was once horrendously fashionable to state, 'Have a nice day', much to the chagrin of most Brits. I feel that this has now been replaced by, 'Please enter your PIN'.

Peter Gibbs
Cranfield, Bedfordshire

SIR – Even the Germans seem to have adopted 'cheers' as an alternative to 'thank you'. On a Lufthansa flight from Frankfurt to Heathrow last week the cabin crew used the word liberally as we left the aeroplane.

They, and we, found it quite amusing.

Jeremy Latham
Winchester, Hampshire

SIR – I'm not surprised that Richard Branson's uniforms are all tits and bums – he never seems to have got over the pubertal excitement of discovering the word *virgin*.

Hugh Bebb
Sunbury-on-Thames, Middlesex

THIS MARRIAGE ISN'T WORKING

SIR – When my teenage niece arrived for lunch yesterday she informed me her friend had been 'Saatchied'.

'She's been what?'

'Saatchied, you know, Saatchied. Her boyfriend Saatchied her and . . .'

Not the type of fame Charles Saatchi would have wanted, but what better punishment?

Maureen Clements
Sible Hedingham, Essex

SIR – Chinning a person in Scotland is known as a Glasgow Kiss. London seems to have found its own riposte in a Saatchi Snog.

Brian Milton
London E2

SIR – If Nigella Lawson had any sense, she would have served Saatchi Weetabix at every meal.

J.R.T.
Exeter

TAUGHT-OROUSLY BAD PUNS

SIR – Surely the headline 'MBE teacher streaked naked' is taught-ologous?

H.E.
Port Erin, Isle of Man

SIR — I read that two villages that have bought their phone box from BT are to undergo a twinning ceremony. Do I take it that they will exchange rings?

R.C.
Bristol

SIR — A picture on the £10 note of Jane Austen 'from behind showing a bit of one cheek' is certainly an interesting thought.

O.H.
Stanway, Essex

SIR — I note in your organ that the incidence of pubic lice has dramatically reduced following the *Sex and the City* effect, which has resulted in a proliferation of Brazilian depilations.

It seems that as we have waxed, they have waned.

J.G. McL.
Newton Abbot, Devon

SIR — I see that Bill Gates is offering up to $1 million to anyone who can re-invent the condom. Do the current products require an updated version with better anti-virus protection?

R.W.
Castle Rising, Norfolk

SIR — Rather than looking for an Indian takeaway dish in Canterbury, perhaps the Archbishop should try to find something more British. Might I suggest the piece of cod that passes all understanding — with chips?

D.R.
Sunningdale, Berkshire

SIR — Is it not time for us to consider that there's no Pope without smoke?

A.M.
Tenterden, Kent

SIR — Now that research has shown that loud music helps plants to bloom, will Black Sabbath be reclassified as a Heavy Petal band?

J.H.
Menston, West Yorkshire

SIR — Are the reports true that one of the offences Rolf Harris is alleged to have committed involved tying a kangaroo down for sport?

C.J.
Llangernyw, Conwy

SIR — In light of Ukip's recent successes I now see why Eric Pickles has been banging on about his 'conserve-a-tory' policy.

> **J. A-S.**
> New York City, USA

SIR — Was Oscar Pistorius refused bail because he might do a runner?

> **D.A.**
> Bacup, Lancashire

SIR — Your correspondent suggests that England might have played in purple because they were sponsored by Quality Street. I certainly noticed some soft centres.

> **P.A.**
> Bodle Street Green, East Sussex

SIR — The only link I could fathom between fashion designer Karl Lagerfeld's cricket creations was that the model has long legs.

> **A.J.**
> Cheltenham, Gloucestershire

SIR — I get increasingly confused by the names of players at Wimbledon. Sometimes I have to think *ova* and *ova* again to decide *vic* is *vic*.

> **M.E.**
> Winchester, Hampshire

SIR — Should next Sunday's final be played between Andy Murray and Novak Djokovic, could it be dubbed: 'The Battle of the Djoks'?

> **F.R.P.**
> Tyldesley, Lancashire

SIR — So, it is definitely Richard III. I wonder if this means that opportunist camping equipment suppliers will announce, 'Now is the discount of our winter tents'.

> **J.G.**
> Ramsbottom, Lancashire

SIR — Would it be possible for Leicester University to check the rumour that Richard III actually said, 'A horse, a horse, my lasagne needs a horse'?

> **G.H.**
> Rodborough Common, Gloucestershire

SIR – Doesn't this suggest that Richard III was a slightly below par-king?

C.R.
Loddisw, Devon

THE ROADS MUCH TRAVELLED

HELMETED HARPIES

SIR — As a mild-mannered and middle-aged
provincial motorist, I was shocked and puzzled
by regular reports of road rage against cyclists
in London. Recently, however, I dropped off a
package to a friend in Peckham and wended my way
through rush-hour traffic out of the capital. Now I
understand perfectly.

At every junction, the motorist is mobbed by
a swarm of two-wheeled, helmeted harpies that
thread their way, mostly unlit, through the traffic,
scraping the sides of the cars until they get to the
front, where they position themselves in front of the
bumper, making quite sure to obstruct the exit from
the lights.

When the lights change, they straggle off at their
own pace. If they time it perfectly, the last one
moves just as the lights turn, causing the motorist
to miss his chance. Before the lights change again, a
new set of harpies arrive.

You eventually get clear of the lights and pass your
tormentors, only for them to catch you at the next
lights. Then it all happens again.

I even noted one bearded individual who found
it necessary to show his complete contempt for all
things motorised by resting his boot on the bumper
of the nearest car at every intersection.

For a while, I was restrained by an anachronistic

and quaintly provincial anxiety not to hurt anybody. Yet by Richmond this impediment had largely worn off and I could have cheerfully mowed down the lot of them. I was only saved from this fate by the blessed sight of a cyclist-free M3.

I support Boris Johnson's pledge to turn London into a cycle-friendly city — anything to clear these anarchic menaces off the main thoroughfares.

Andy Lyons
Thornford, Dorset

SIR — On my walk home this evening through central London I had to give way, at various points, to three cyclists at zebra crossings and three others who had ignored a red light. For three more who had foregone the roads altogether I was an inconvenient obstacle on the pavement.

When did this casual law-breaking become the norm? And why does quietly pointing it out merit abuse rather than an apology?

It is not as if they were all on Boris bikes and therefore mandated to ride like clowns.

Andrew Shapland
London SW8

SURVIVING A SIXTIES NIGHT BUS

SIR — You report that a woman has accused a DJ of putting his hand up her skirt. To me that was small beer. I was frequently treated far worse on public transport — especially when climbing the stairs on omnibuses.

This was in the late fifties, early sixties, and for a while it was frightening for me. Many fellow passengers just smirked — even the women — so I developed my own form of punishment.

I found the best deterrent was a pair of stiletto heels and an umbrella with a nice sharp ferrule. A quick step backwards and a judicious prod when alighting gave me great satisfaction. The men could not cry out in pain, and learned never to sit by me again.

Friends always wondered why I always carried an umbrella, even in the height of summer, and they often saw why when going home on the last bus with me.

Ann Thompson
Paignton, Devon

JOURNEYS IN THE SMOG OF 1952

SIR – On the evening of Saturday December 6, 1952, I was one of a group of stagehands outside the Old Vic Theatre. Killing time before the interval, we watched as ambulances from their headquarters in Waterloo Road were led through the murk by men carrying flares.

In the distance we heard a bus on the far side of the road approaching from the left. A moment later we also heard a car on the same side, travelling in the wrong direction.

The driver must have heard us talking and called out: 'Am I alright for Purley?'

One of our chaps replied: 'Hang on there, mate, and you'll see the gates in a moment.'

Douglas Cornelissen
Shenley, Hertfordshire

SIR – One of my colleagues lived at Reading. Going home in 1952, he found Paddington station in some despair. However, there was a train waiting – first stop Reading.

He thought to see if food was available on the train and had a leisurely three-course dinner. It was only when looking out after dinner that he discovered that the train had still not left. He alighted and found a hotel for the night.

As he put it, if he had known, he would not have chosen to dine in a train in Paddington station.

Ian Macpherson
Guildford, Surrey

SIR – I attended a London wedding on December 6, 1952. As Best Man tasked with getting my friend to the altar of Holy Trinity, Brompton, we awaited the bride's arrival with increasing concern, heightened by the fog seeping steadily into the building and obscuring our view of the main entrance.

Against the odds we gathered a full complement of guests, including a Catholic party who thought they were at a nearby wedding at Brompton Oratory.

After the reception, the ushers and I escorted the bridesmaids out on the town. The only means of transport was the Underground and the fog was so thick down there that on emerging we noticed that the girls' décolletages were thickly etched with grime and everyone's hair was full of soot.

J.C.
Rudgwick, West Sussex

THE NORTH SOUTH TANNOY DIVIDE

SIR – As I commence my weekly commute from Durham to Reading, the station Tannoy states that 'unattended items will be removed by the Transport Police'. Five hours later the Reading announcement warns that 'all unattended items will be removed and destroyed by the Security Services'.

Is this an example of pretentious southern self-aggrandisement or a warranted step up in the agency dealing with security?

Mark Goff
Reading

SIR – Some years ago, travelling on the train from London to Liverpool, the announcement came through that, 'For the convenience of our passengers, the buffet car is now closed.' The resulting comments in a carriage full of returning Scousers could have scripted a half-hour comedy show.

Alan Chester
Crosby, Merseyside

SIR – I will never forget that, when travelling from Winchester to Waterloo a few years ago, the guard announced, 'Passengers wishing to know what it is like to suffer from depression should alight at the next station, Basingstoke.'

The train was pretty full and we all collapsed with laughter.

Michael Elton
Winchester, Hampshire

SIR – I have always been irritated and amused by the tautology, 'Would passengers be sure to take all their personal belongings with them.' It makes me wonder what my impersonal belongings might look like.

Robin Lane
Devizes, Wiltshire

SIR – My favourite announcement was on the London Underground. The train was stationary at Green Park because in the words of the guard, 'There are no trains ahead of us and no trains behind us, so we are being held here to regulate the service.'

R.G.
Sutton-at-Hone, Kent

SIR – President Obama's phrase in his inauguration address that 'our journey is not complete' would play well to British train commuters were he ever to make a pitch for political office in the UK.

Keith Flett
London N17

LOW-SPEED JAZZ

SIR — It's a perfect evening on the borders of Northamptonshire, Oxfordshire and Warwickshire. There is not a breath of air and a mile away a lonely pigeon calls, 'Come find me' to her mate. The only unnatural sounds are a 747 heading for Heathrow at 35,000 feet and the tinkle of after-dinner jazz.

This idyll is repeated along the 100 miles between London and Birmingham. Can't someone stop the craziness of the HS2 project which will destroy the lives of all of us who live along the route?

Simon Moss
Lower Boddington, Northamptonshire

SIR — In the world of high-speed trains, who is to provide the replacement bus service? Ferrari?

Steve Cattell
Hougham, Lincolnshire

SIR — The biggest disadvantage of high-speed rail is that we will have less time to admire the beauty of wind turbines.

Brian Christley
Abergele, Conwy

SIR — We need more water in the south and the suggestion is that it be supplied from the north. Surely a water pipe could be incorporated into the HS2 project, with each train generating a pressure wave as it goes south?

Geoff Knott
Dorking, Surrey

SIR — If the water companies in the south bring down water from the north, will our beer taste better?

Robert Ballantine
Chevington, Suffolk

ROAD OVER-KILL

SIR — Why do we need a badger cull? Most of them seem to be already dead at the side of our roads.

Alexis Howard
Chartham Hatch, Kent

SIR – Spotted yesterday on the M40: a sporty
vehicle being driven by a heavily bearded young man
with the registration T4LBAN.

N. Sussames
Mundford, Norfolk

THE ROADS TO DIVORCE

SIR – Your article about map-reading arguments
leading to divorce reminded me of a marriage which
has also sadly ended, although probably not due
only to cartographic differences.

While driving through London and arguing over
the best route, the couple were crossing a bridge
over the Thames. The wife, infuriated by her
husband's intransigence, wound down the window
and hurled the *A to Z* into the river, shouting: 'Now
you can go whichever way you want to.'

Maybe sat-nav systems have helped to reduce
divorce levels?

Ian Brent-Smith
Bicester, Oxfordshire

SIR — My wife is an excellent map-reader. Her directions, such as, 'You should have turned right back there', are unerringly accurate.

> **P.F.**
> Coulsdon, Surrey

SIR — I am pleased to report that my wife and I survived a journey of over 3,400km last year with only three map-reading errors. That said, if I am to be in the car when my wife drives, I have to be in the boot.

> **J.P.**
> Puesta del Sol, Spain

SIR — I was an early adopter of the sat nav in 1998 when I had a splendid Audi Estate with one of the first in-built units.

It had an amazing ability to change languages. Olga's commands were short, and to the point: 'Links! Recht!' Françoise, on the other hand, was often quite petulant, while the wonderful Francesca issued her instructions so volubly that one was half a mile past the intersection before she had finished her lecture.

I adored her, and so did a couple of visiting Indian businessmen, who rocked with laughter as we went round a roundabout five times on the outskirts of Liverpool to see if she could regain her composure.

She could not, and went silent for the rest of the day.

Robert Hill
Irby, Wirral

VISITING DEAR OLD LONDON

SIR — I visited London recently. We seem to have the dearest fare in the world for a short journey on the Underground. We also have some of the most expensive petrol, gas, electricity, rail fares, aviation taxes and road taxes in the Western world. Meanwhile, our roads are nearing the standard of those we used to see in Eastern Europe.

Are we getting value for money?

Howard Stevens
Norton, County Durham

PS The chances of getting a letter published are pretty low, but writing to the *Telegraph* lets off steam. If and when the press is 'regulated' my only hope will be to write: 'What a good job our ministers are doing with the economy — bravely pursuing our Green Agenda.'

SIR – While travelling on the Underground recently I accidentally made momentary eye contact with a sullen-looking hooded youth sprawled on the opposite seat. He wasn't happy with this and leaned forward (rather too close) and said, 'Have you gotta problem?' in a tone of voice that implied I very soon would have.

To my relief (and clearly that of nearby passengers) his stop arrived and he got off, informing me I was '****ing lucky' as he left.

Can any reader suggest a reply that would have averted unpleasant escalation of this encounter, had he stayed put?

Geoff Chessum
London EC2

SIR – I have just returned from a long weekend in London which was ruined by so many well-mannered teenagers leaping up to offer me their seats on the Tube. The feeling of being young, energetic and sprightly, which I had before I went up to the capital, has been completely dashed.

Ron Kirby
Dorchester, Dorest

SIR – I can sympathise with Ian McEwan not finding the countryside what he expected. I recently bought

a town house in London for my weekend visits.
I was very upset to discover that I cannot park my
car outside and that the street lights are on all night.
Even worse, there is not a decent pheasant shoot
for miles.

Steve Davis
Bromsash, Herefordshire

SIR — Now that it is open to the public, I will gladly
pay £25 to visit the observation deck at the Shard
for the same reason that Guy de Maupassant ate his
lunch each day in the Eiffel Tower's restaurant. It
was the only vantage point in the city from which the
hated landmark was not visible.

Charlie Voss
London W14

HOME THOUGHTS ON ABROAD

FAST FALLIBILITY

SIR — It's Lent, and Benedict XVI has given up being the Pope. I challenge anyone to top that.

Donald Keir
Aberdeen

SIR — When the Pope retires from office at the end of the month will he become fallible again like the rest of us?

John Peck
Harpenden, Hertfordshire

SIR — The BBC tells us, 'The world is stunned' by the resignation of the Pope. I would like to confirm I am mildly surprised at best.

Jonathan Fulford
Bosham, West Sussex

SIR — Famously, in 1944, the words *Utah*, *Juno*, *Gold*, *Sword* and *Omaha* — all codenames for D-Day beaches — appeared as solutions in *The Daily Telegraph*'s crossword. *Overlord*, codename for the whole D-Day operation, appeared on May 27 and *Neptune*, codename for the naval assault phase, on June 1.

On Saturday Feb 9, 2013, the Pub Quiz in the *Telegraph* Weekend section contained the following question: 'Celestine V in 1294 is the only man in history to abdicate which title?'

Is there something you should tell us?

M.D.
Patching, West Sussex

SIR — May I say how saddened I was on reading the English translation of the Pope's resignation declaration to find it contained a split infinitive?

John Letchford
Elsenham, Hertfordshire

SIR — At least Jesus didn't quit.

D.W.
Long Crendon, Buckinghamshire

SIR — I wonder if Pope Benedict has considered retiring to Avignon.

Ronnie Maclean
Cumbernauld, Lanarkshire

SIR — Under Dilnot would the Pope have to sell the Sistine Chapel to fund his care into old age?

Nick Wray
Winchester, Hampshire

BUMS ON SEATS

SIR — *Sede vacante* has not always been connected with the death of a Pope. When I was growing up in the 1970s we would use the expression at home to denote that the bathroom was free.

Andrew Holmes
Bromley, Kent

SIR — A golden opportunity presents itself to appoint Tony Blair as Pope. This would, at a stroke, give him the power he craves and remove a number of his other ambitions.

Tim Page
Downton, Wiltshire

SIR — Wouldn't it be wonderful if the new Pope revived the crusading activities of his forebears?

Robert Rodrigo
Burwell, Cambridgeshire

SIR — Surely the ideal candidate would be Professor Brian Cox? He appears to be omniscient, ubiquitous and he has the face of a cherub.

Peter Etherton
Wellington, Somerset

SIR – Could the solution to two problems be solved at a single stroke: an Italian returned to the Holy See; the Italian people protected against more international ridicule? And surely, following his expensive divorce, Silvio Berlusconi could even satisfy the requirement for celibacy?

Simon Edsor
London SW1

SIR – Should Cardinal Angelo Scola be elected Pope I see a conflict of interest with a certain soft drinks company.

Dominic Shelmerdine
London W8

SIR – I see we now have bookmakers offering odds on the election of a new Pope. I fear it will not be long now before they open the betting on the date of the Second Coming. Is nothing sacred anymore?

Richard Mann
Bideford, Devon

SIR – May I thank you for the excellent coverage of the election of the new Pope. May I suggest, however, that the layout of page eight was less than appropriate. The juxtaposition of shapely bottoms

and ladies panties, even from the saintly Marks &
Spencer, does not fit well with the dignity of the
Papal office.

C.B.
Torquay, Devon

SIR – Now that we have an Argentinean Pope
who is also a Jesuit, does this mean that the
Holy Inquisition will invade the Falkland
Islands?

Roy Bailey
Great Shefford, Berkshire

SIR – Someone should remind the new Pope what
happened the last time a Pope encouraged a sea-
borne invasion of a British island.

John Crooks
London SW15

THE MAU MAU TAPESTRY

SIR – The British Government has announced
compensation of £20 million to Kenya. As a direct
descendant of King Harold can I now claim against
the Ministry of Defence for failing to provide my
ancestor with effective anti-arrow eye protection?

If not, I am prepared to accept an apology from the Prime Minister.

Major Malcolm Allen (retd)
Berkhamsted, Hertfordshire

SIR – As Mr Cameron has accepted responsibility for the Amritsar massacre he must resign.

Brian Gilbert
Hampton, Middlesex

SIR – Oh, for goodness sake, it is bad enough that the Government has taken to making hand-wringing apologies for slavery and other ancient misdemeanours that are now viewed through the rose-tinted spectacles of today's dripping-wet politically correct.

Now we are being told not to mention the fact that the bloody Huns started the First World War (and the Second World War, while we're on the subject of mass slaughter).

I'm off to tune up the Merlins on the Lancaster. Anyone care to join me?

Robert Warner
West Woodhay, Berkshire

SIR – Your correspondent, a press officer for Haworth 1940s Weekend, tries to explain away the appearance of people dressed up as Nazis as 'hobbyists who seek to be as accurate as possible'.

The most accurate re-enactment for these so-called hobbyists would be to shoot them down in flames.

In view of the shortage of Messerschmitts, I can only suggest that other hobbyists, dressed as Home Guards, should round them up at the point of a bayonet and take them to the nearest police station to be locked up for the duration of the weekend.

Richard Shaw
Dunstable, Bedfordshire

SIR — Is there a connection between the flooding in Germany and this being the 70th anniversary of the Dambusters raid?

Group Captain Terry Holloway (retd)
Great Wratting, Suffolk

JUDGING JOHNNY FOREIGNER

SIR — General Adrian Carton de Wiart VC, whose military records you published today, escaped in 1939 from the German invasion of Poland with a group of Polish pilots. While travelling through Romania they were betrayed to the Germans. Of the natives of Romania, the General later wrote in his autobiography: 'Pimps, pederasts and violinists — and very few of them play the violin.'

Jeremy M.J. Havard
London SW3

SIR — I was told many times by my father that the Italians were a nation of gigolos and comedians. He has now been proved correct on both fronts.

Colin Perkins
Hutton, Essex

SIR — So, Italy has elected a comedian. We have a government full of them.

Patrick Brennan
Stevington, Bedfordshire

SIR — Was it really necessary to publish pictures of Angela Merkel in her swimsuit? What next, David Cameron in a mankini?

Alex Smith
Orford, Suffolk

SIR — There is obviously a fundamental difference between the Russian and the English psyches.

In Russia the bare-chested President (or is he

Prime Minister?) wrestles bears and carries them home on his shoulder. In England the Prime Minister wears wellies and rescues a sheep from a muddy pond.

It's very comforting.

A.G. Mordey
Lillington, Warwickshire

SNOWDEN'S FACEBOOK FRIENDS

SIR – On Sunday July 7 I posted the following on Facebook: 'What a day! The Lions win the series. Froome is in the yellow jersey. Murray is in the final. Abu Qatada is on a plane to Jordan. Holidays are imminent. The sun is shining. The lark is on the wing. God is in his heaven and all is right in the world.'

Imagine my surprise when this appeared almost word for word as the opening paragraph to Jeremy Warner's column in the *Telegraph* on July 9. Amazing coincidence or something sinisterly Snowden-esque?

David Kilroy
Epsom, Surrey

SIR – Shock and horror! Our spies are spying
on people!

Steve Cartridge
Egerton, Lancashire

SIR – Given that the whole world and his neighbour
knows full well what spooks do, it makes you wonder
to what lengths the Government will go to in order
to conceal the really serious stuff.

Liam Power
Bangor Erris, Co Mayo

SIR – I am sure Edward Snowden would be very
welcome in North Korea.

Don Roberts
Birkenhead, Wirral

SIR – Every time I see a photo of Alex Salmond
he looks more and more like the leader of
North Korea. Is it possible that they are one
and the same?

Robert Constant-Taylor
Harrietsham, Kent

SIR — Judging by the chaos in my local supermarket on Saturday, I could only surmise that North Korea's threats were being taken seriously.

Paul Wilson
Little Canfield, Essex

WRESTLING WITH EGYPT

SIR — I, for one, would hesitate before disputing anything with Adly Mansour, the interim President of Egypt. Should times become hard for him, he looks as though he is physically equipped to become a successful sumo competitor.

Dr John Gladstone
Gerrards Cross, Buckinghamshire

SIR — Watching what is happening in Egypt, I can now see why our Armed Forces have been reduced and weakened so dramatically.

Steve Cattell
Hougham, Lincolnshire

SIR — Further to Tony Blair's calls for intervention in Syria, I recently came across a footnote quoting Lieutenant General Napier in the Victorian children's book *Jackanapes*.

General Napier asks: 'What manner of men be they who have supplied the Caffres with the firearms and ammunition to maintain their savage and deplorable wars? Assuredly, they are not military.'

At the risk of confusing literary sources, I fear Tony Blair is in danger of tilting at windmills yet again, at the expense of others' lives.

Donald Marsh
London N19

SIR – The list of important dates for our children in today's *Telegraph* omitted both world wars but included the election of Tony Blair. Is this because the authors considered this last event more devastating to this island of ours than either of the wars?

Peter Thompson
Sutton, Surrey

THE GELATO DEFICIT

SIR – After hearing that a British family were charged £54 for a round of ice creams in Italy, am I alone in thinking that perhaps the likes of Greece should take up such a tactic?

Edward Bunn
Newcastle

SIR — Was it that long ago that one would see
Russians queuing for hours in the streets to buy one
of the few loaves available from the baker?
Now they're queuing up to buy Cyprus.

Paul Vicefield
London N2

SIR — Look on the bright side: at least Cyprus won't
vote for Germany in the Eurovision Song Contest
this year.

Julie Clayton
Malvern, Worcestershire

RADIO AND TELEVISION

CHANNEL FLOPPING

SIR — You report that the average time spent watching television has increased to four and a half hours a day per person. I suspect that this is due to the time spent flicking through the channels trying to find something decent to watch.

Alex Smith
Orford, Suffolk

SIR — I see that this afternoon the BBC is showing a programme called *Pointless Celebrities*. Is there any other kind?

Lt Col John Landau (retd)
Cheltenham, Gloucestershire

SIR — Am I alone in noticing that the programme about the Rolling Stones on Saturday night was followed by a film called *Night of the Living Dead*?

Brendon Chappell
Bexhill-on-Sea, East Sussex

SIR — Am I alone in wishing for an episode of *Countryfile* in which a presenter's offer to 'lend a hand' is turned down?

Andrew Blake
Shalbourne, Wiltshire

SIR — Is it possible to interview people or present a television programme while your hands are not moving?

Robert Vincent
Wildhern, Hampshire

SIR — I am fed up with watching Monty Don walk up and down his garden with his wheelbarrow. In one programme alone I counted 12 journeys.

I also question the value of seeing Monty rolling around in his pond liner with Jo Swift.

And how many times are we to be shown how to plant bulbs and sow seeds? It's on the packet.

Maggie Down
Paulerspury, Northamptonshire

SIR — The BBC promises a young and devilishly handsome Edward VI in its new drama about the War of the Roses. He must be very young when you consider he wasn't born until more than 50 years after the war ended.

Les Sharp
Hersham, Surrey

SIR — Do the Danes prefer *Midsomer Murders* to *The Killing* because more people are murdered in a single episode than in the whole series of *The Killing*? Or do they like the simple format, in which Inspector Barnaby finally arrests the only person still alive, on the basis that he or she must be the murderer?

> **Brian Christley**
> Abergele, Conwy

SIR – After watching episodes seven and eight of *Borgen* my wife turned to me and said: 'I wish Birgitte Nyborg was our Prime Minister.'

> **Peter Roberts**
> Exeter

SIR – Whether the setting is the courts, a police station, Westminster or a village – and whether the theme is dramatic or comedic – commissioning editors at the BBC show a marked preference for plots featuring sassy female leads and a supporting male cast of misogynist, insensitive dullards.

All a bit sexist, don't you think?

> **Jerry Gosney**
> Rotherfield, East Sussex

SIR – Yes, mumbling actors are very annoying, but could I make a plea to restrict the use of the distant, barking dogs so often used to create atmosphere in drama? All this does is arouse my dog from his sleep on the sofa, setting off a spate of barking which makes it even more difficult to understand the actors.

James Logan
Portstewart, Co Londonderry

SIR — I long held a theory that should anyone wish to find out the state of this country, they had only to watch a few editions of *The Jeremy Kyle Show*. I have now had a shift of opinion. We should watch *The Apprentice*.

Harry Page
Arley, Worcestershire

LEARNING TO SPEAK DOWNTON PEDANT

SIR — Further to 'learning curve', I'm pretty sure I heard the Dowager Countess say 'parenting' in *Downton Abbey*. Some mistake, surely?

James Barraclough
Stansted, Essex

SIR — *Downton Abbey* has got it wrong again. When the train left the station, the semaphore signal was up. Until after the Second World War, the signal for a clear track ahead was down. It was changed to up for safety purposes. The heritage line officials should have told them.

Chris Harding
Parkstone, Dorset

SIR – Christmas was ruined by the *Downton Abbey* special. The women were distraught at the demise of Matthew Crawley, while the men were more concerned about the possibly irreparable damage to his car.

Cynthia Dunn
Rhosllanerchrugog, Wrexham

SIR – With all the furore regarding the errors in *Downton Abbey*, might I enquire, in view of the few cars that were on the road in those days, what were the chances of two vehicles crashing – let alone at a sufficient speed to cause a fatality?

Susan Lister
West Horndon, Essex

SIR – I note the lettering on Matthew Crawley's gravestone in the picture in today's *Daily Telegraph* has been engraved in Times New Roman. Crawley died in 1921; the typeface was not launched until the early 1930s.

I also see that the italic has been optically

italicised — this a very recent possibility.

Let's have some typographic verisimilitude in our historical dramas.

Derek Cross
Brenchley, Kent

SIR — Maybe the writers drop such anachronisms into the script in the hope of getting a response. Their own amusing Christmas game, perhaps?

Dominic Weston Smith
Fernham, Oxfordshire

SIR — I entirely agree with Serena Davies's eulogy to 'the finest actor in *Downton Abbey*', the 'mesmerisingly charismatic' Dan Stevens.

He did not 'work against the text' as lesser actors might have done, but stayed true to Julian Fellowes's dialogue. Hand in hand, both masters of their craft, Stevens created the most impressive evocation of a nice, but insuperably dull, person I have seen, never allowing the absence of that essential feature of the dashing hero — cheekbones — to stand in his way.

A long, thoughtful stare into the abyss of impotency, counter-balanced by the stiffness of his upper lip; a subtle tightening of the jaw or narrowing of the eyes — never both together — at the suffering in the trenches and the loss of a dinner-jacket; tiny clues which found us working furiously for the inner meaning.

Anne Chamberlain
Romiley, Cheshire

CRITICISING THE CRITICS

SIR — Last night I watched ITV's new comedy, *Vicious*, because the *Sunday Telegraph*'s television critic said, 'ITV has a comedy hit on its hands at last'. This morning's *Telegraph* TV critic declared it 'the least funny comedy in recent memory'.

Am I to ignore the critics?

Paul Chapman
Wirral

SIR — If your critic found *Tomorrow's World* too difficult all I can say is: hard cheese. I am 94 and I found it excellent. She must be just the sort of viewer for whom the all-too-common voiceovers — 'Michael Portillo is now walking along the station platform' — for tiny tots are designed.

Michael Holden
East Chiltington, East Sussex

SIR – Your critic describes plasma physics as a 'ridiculously named specialism'. I would be fascinated to hear her suggestion for a less ridiculous term to describe the physics of plasmas, by far the most common phase of ordinary matter found in the known universe.

Dr Simon Richards CPhys FInstP
Newton, Dorset

FRY BY THE LORRY-LOAD

SIR – At last, Stephen Pollard has given me my 'Am I alone in thinking . . .?' chance! How grateful I am that some other human being has come blinking into the light to question the continual exposure we are forced to face to the assorted works of Stephen Fry.

I know that, for the BBC, this view may be as close to heresy as it is possible to get, but there are those of us, we happy few, who are thoroughly bored with the cult of Mr Fry.

Learned and witty he may be – and he does a cracking turn in *Blackadder* – but, as Mr Pollard says, 'Enough!' Get thee hence, Mr Fry, and do not darken our doors until many moons have passed.

And as for Clare ******* Balding!

Yours in a tizz,
James Munro
Ashurst Wood, West Sussex

SIR — Watched the BBC coverage of Margaret
Thatcher's funeral. Couldn't believe it — no Clare
Balding. Where was she?

Richard Allison
Newport

RADIO SILENCE

SIR — I understood my wife's meaning but was a
little bemused when, at 10.50am on Remembrance
Day, she said, 'Darling, put on the radio so we can
listen to the two-minute silence.'

Well, of course I did, and we did, and we
always will.

John Dominy
Kentisbeare, Devon

SIR — Each morning my wife and I switch on our
radios. Hers, a new DAB radio, is consistently two-
and-a-half pips late on my old-fashioned FM one.

Surely mine cannot be wrong; it has been giving
the time for over 30 years, whereas the DAB radio is
a newcomer to this exacting skill.

Which of us is losing two-and-a-half seconds of
life each day?

Christopher Pole-Carew
Axminster, Devon

SIR – Rarely has the BBC had a more suitable candidate for banishment to its desert island than Julie Burchill. It is a refreshing thought that her incarceration will not be helped by her appalling choice of music.

Michael Toynbee
Amberley, West Sussex

BOMBING BORCHESTER

SIR – Some years ago I was a member of the BBC Listeners' Panel. Once, wonderfully, we were asked to suggest a script for *The Archers*. I had no hesitation in suggesting the neutron bomb be tested in Borchester.

Robert Henshcr
London W1

SIR – Debate about *The Archers* is superfluous. It was cancelled some years ago, and replaced by a tiresome *EastEnders* soundalike.

Eugene Smith
Harrow, Middlesex

THOUGHTS FOR TODAY

SIR — We can all congratulate Mishal Husain on her appointment to the *Today* programme but, equally, what a pity that another extremely well-educated person ends up in the media or politics — hardly productive professions.

Michael Edwards
Haslemere, Surrey

SIR — The delight of regular listeners to the *Today* programme at the addition of a young woman to the presenter team will be complete if the opportunity is taken to retire both James Naughtie, whose rambling questions are often longer than the answers, and John Humphrys, who is long past his sell-by date.

And dare one hope that the new recruit reads your newspaper, and not just the *Guardian* like the present gang?

Major Colin Robins
Bowdon, Cheshire

DEAR *DAILY*
TELEGRAPH

DISGUSTED OF SURREY

SIR — Saturday's edition featured six letters from Surrey. Please do not repeat this phenomenon. It's bad enough telling people you live in Surrey, as the rest of the world assumes we are all bankers or stockbrokers. Now they will think we have nothing better to do than read the papers and write to the editor.

Lyn Chalcraft
Cranleigh, Surrey

SIR — The 'editor', whoever the **** is, never acknowledges anything I write. He is so stuck up the ***** of pensioners in Sussex that anyone who knows anything about anything may as well **** into the wind.

Dr A.G. BSc (Hons) PhD MRICS
Barsby, Leicestershire

SIR — My morning ritual: look for Matt, put on the kettle, scan the letters page, smile if I am included, call you a silly b****** if I am not, try the crossword (more swearing), make a cuppa, then I am ready for the day to begin.

K.B.
Englefield Green, Surrey

SIR — Every time you publish a letter from someone from Moreton-in-Marsh I award myself £5 towards a day at Cheltenham races. Today you have added £10 to my pot.

Mark Coote
Alvescot, Oxfordshire

SIR — I don't read your paper very often, but whenever I do, it seems that I am guaranteed to find: 1) a story in which a rich landowner is complaining about his property being 'blighted' by an actual or proposed wind turbine; and 2) a letter complaining about wind turbines.

Can I ask: is this a mere coincidence? Or does it constitute general editorial policy?

J.D.
Tunbridge Wells, Kent

SIR — What do 100 'academics' actually do when they're not writing to *The Daily Telegraph*?

Jasper Archer
Stapleford, Wiltshire

SIR — The *Telegraph* is always telling us we need to be more efficient. I was disappointed therefore that yesterday you printed two letters about Chris Huhne, one demanding the return of his salary, the other demanding the return of his severance pay.

Both these demands were made in the one letter I sent, a 50 per cent increase in productivity.

Ian Birchall
Burn Bridge, North Yorkshire

SIR — While browsing through your latest delightful volume of unpublished letters, I notice that you fear running out of titles for future annual volumes in this, I hope, enduring series. May I suggest: *Oh Dear, Oh Dear, Oh Dear . . .*, which is often my reaction when reading news items, letters or articles in *The Daily Telegraph*, and expresses my exasperation at the views being aired.

Rear Admiral J.A.L. Myres
Dorchester-on-Thames, Oxfordshire

PS I've rather given up writing letters for publication, as it is clear that, for a luddite like myself who does not have email, there is little chance of striking the appropriate chord with the letters page sifters. Never mind — it was fun while it lasted.

I even have one framed in my 'loo', together with the cartoon upon which I was commenting. Little things please little minds.

DELIGHTED OF LLANBRYNMAIR

SIR — I have been published on my birthday, and I am not even hyphenated. My wife has bought me *I Could Go On . . .*, *Imagine My Surprise . . .* and *I Rest My Case . . .* as presents.

What joy! It cannot get any better.

Den Beves
Llanbrynmair, Powys

SIR — Apart from the joy and excitement of seeing one's letter published in a national newspaper (especially the *Telegraph*), the question is: what to do with them? My answer has been to make them into an artistic collage of what (lack of) imagination I have.

James A. Paton
Billericay, Essex

SIR — My delight at your acceptance of my letter turned into absolute amazement when I read your paper this morning before setting off to visit family in Scotland. Barry Hubbard, who is my next-door neighbour and friend, had written independently on the same topic. We had not seen each other for several days.

The odds on this happening must be astronomical.

Commander Alan York (retd)
Sheffield

SIR – One of the pleasures of reading the letters in your newspaper is to be reminded of the variety and romance of English village names. Today's offerings are a good example. You have correspondents from Netherne on the Hill, Gladestry, Micheldever, Nanstallon and Chale. Long may that continue.

D.M.
Surbiton, Surrey

SIR – After years of trying without success, I may have appeared in your letters column by default.

Often I meet ladies walking dogs in the Oswestry area, and it is my habit to touch my cap when encountering them. I do hope it's me to whom your correspondent is referring.

B. Slater
Pontfadog, Wrexham

SIR – Following your publication of my letter about the state of our village telephone box I was called the next day by a BT representative who confirmed that it has now been scheduled for repainting and refurbishment.

Once again, this proves the power of the *Telegraph*'s letters page.

Paul Strong
Claxby, Lincolnshire

SIR — After sending an email to the *Telegraph* containing the words, 'Eastern European migrant worker' I was immediately shown an advertisement by Google Mail offering me a cleaning job in Oxford.

Simon Leadbeater
Benson, Oxfordshire

THE DAILY ADVERTISER

SIR — Might I suggest that you rename your paper the *Daily Advertiser* — or at least lower its price — until after Christmas? I can view broadsheet portraits of Brad Pitt in my granddaughter's room, should I wish to do so.

Sid King
Felden, Hertfordshire

THE TROLL WALL

SIR — Instead of charging people to read your excellent articles on the internet, you should ask for a small subscription if they wish to leave a comment. You would make just as much money, dump all the trolls and generally spread sweetness and light.

Neville Nicholson
Haverhill, Suffolk

CRYSTAL BALLS

SIR — Your racing tipster's advice on Auroras Encore, the Grand National winner, was: 'Poor jumper and odds-on not to reach the finish.'

The tipster needs a new job, but please do not move him to the financial pages.

Luke Grant
Pensax Common, Worcestershire

SIR — Why is it that whenever you have an article about forthcoming weather on the front page, it is always different from the forecast on the back page?

Today you report that snowstorms are expected. On the back page we have simply 'a period of rain'.

Time will tell which is correct, but I have to make a journey on Sunday.

Stuart Gordon
Nottingham

SIR – Imagine my thrill when I read that as a *Telegraph* reader, I could win a kindling bucket and a matchbox. And I can't wait to stand up to my nose in snow with my traction treads, de-icing salt and US Army torch.

Does the *Telegraph* know something we don't?

Joseph G. Dawson
Withnell, Lancashire

RIP, PATRICK MOORE

SIR – In Sir Patrick Moore's obituary mention is made of a scar he had over his eye as a result of a motorcycle accident in 1952. That happened outside our house. My mother made him a cup of tea, which he drank while he waited for the ambulance.

Fifty years later, when I met him at a book signing, he asked fondly after my mother.

Barry Jackson
Tadley, Hampshire

SIR – Shortly after leaving the RAF, Patrick Moore arrived at St Andrew's School, Woking, a boys' prep school owned by my father, Walsham Maynard. Here he taught history, maths and French with exuberance and flair.

On one occasion he suggested that my mother might like to have a look at the stars of the night sky. My mother was extremely surprised when the focus of the telescope suddenly moved from the planets to the house next door, where the resident Land Girls were undressing.

He travelled everywhere by motorbike, owning two at that time, one called Stromboli and the other Vesuvius. Lessons were never quite so exciting after he left to pursue his real passion, but he remained in touch with us throughout his life.

Gabrielle Robertson
Carpow, Perthshire

SIR – Patrick Moore was my French teacher in 1952, when I was a seven-year-old pupil at Holmewood House Prep School near Tunbridge Wells.

I was hopeless, and he knew it. My first French essay was returned with no actual mark, but just the word 'Ass!' written large in red ink across the first page.

Three years later I was delighted to win his novel *Island of Fear* as first prize for English Language. It was signed, and I've treasured it to this day.

Eccentric, brilliant, a wonderful communicator and, best of all, what a character.

David Darley
Cove, Hampshire

RED-TOP JOURNALISM

SIR — I read with little interest your piece on Prince Harry's follicle challenge. Should we look forward to interviews with *Big Brother* contestants or, perhaps, Boris Johnson bare-breasted on page three?

Robin Kemp
Smeeton Westerby, Leicestershire

SIR — I am so relieved that Carol Vorderman's nose has healed. It is worth paying £1.20 for that alone, and the experience is enhanced by the knowledge that a reporter has braved a trawl of the internet to find a tweet.

James Patrick
London N10

SIR — So, the Duke and Duchess argue over scrabble. If you really have no news you should just print fewer pages.

Russell Payne
Tunbridge Wells, Kent

SIR — I challenge you to produce just one edition of *The Daily Telegraph* which doesn't mention *Downton Abbey*.

Susan Bownass
Yelling, Cambridgeshire

SIR — Max Davidson writes that he gained happiness when he turned off his phone. He will be even happier if he does not read a newspaper (but I bet *The Daily Telegraph* will not print this).

Loris Goring
Brixham, Devon

DIRTY NEWS

SIR — Your correspondent has little to praise himself based on obtaining applause for being the only man who washed his hands after the 'event', as this carries the strong implication that he pees on his fingers.

As someone who has a frugal lunch, plus a pint, accompanied by *The Daily Telegraph*, I always find it necessary to wash my hands *before* going to the lavatory, because of your newspaper's dirty print coming off on my hands.

Michael Ward
London SW19

I AM NOT ALONE

SIR – In answer to the classic *Telegraph* reader's question, 'Am I alone in thinking . . .?' I find in today's opinion pages not just one but two illustrations that I am not. Thank you, Stephen Pollard and Philip Johnston.

Robert Quayle
West Drayton, Middlesex

SIR – My telephone call today to the *Telegraph* was answered almost instantaneously by a live human voice. I was so stunned it left me momentarily speechless.

My query was passed to the relevant department and a most helpful young man, who just happens to live in the same village as me, dealt with it very efficiently.

100 per cent customer satisfaction.

Ursula Gilmore
Bearsted, Kent

SIR – How much I enjoy reading my copy of *The Daily Telegraph*, no more so than today! This feeling of comfort is almost certainly due to the fact that one tends to agree with the views expressed by your correspondents and the many varied letter writers.

On reflection, this consensus is really most unsatisfactory because it is preaching to the converted. How can we spread these sensible and logical views more widely?

R.D. Ambrose
London SW13

SIR – I received a copy of *I Rest My Case . . .* as a Christmas present. While perusing this I am sure you can 'imagine my surprise' when I read that one of your correspondents purchased his newspaper 'from the local Co-op'. Prior to this I had assumed that your erudite broadsheet was available only from such as Waitrose.

May I commend you on your success at reaching out to a wider population. Long may this trend continue.

Paul Strong
Claxby, Lincolnshire

iRUSTLE

SIR — My change to reading the *Telegraph* on the iPad has put a stop to my wife's once familiar daggers look at me, followed by her turning up the volume of the television. However, I do wish the iPad edition had the option of a crinkling page-turning noise so that now and again I could remind her of what she's missing.

Stephen Gledhill
Chadbury, Worcestershire

SIR — As well as rattling the pages of his *Telegraph* at a considerable speed, my husband generates a gale-force wind in my direction. I retaliate with my *Daily Mail* in the opposite direction. We are now considering how we can harness all this extra power.

Jennifer Graeme
Ringmore, Devon

SIR — I will gladly cease my page rattling if my wife will ensure that, once she has had her fill, our *Telegraph* is back in its original condition and not folded with the crossword forward.

Ian Wearing
Welwyn, Hertfordshire

CROSS WORDS

SIR – Am I alone in my frustration at the occasional full back-page advertisement displacing your crossword? On such days I struggle to open and fold your august organ before I can commence battle, bearing scant attention to whatever is being touted.

This is a waste of advertising space, a backward step for the back page.

R.R.B.
Dartmouth, Devon

SIR – Question: when is a general knowledge crossword not a general knowledge crossword? Answer: when virtually all the questions relate in some way to the Olympics.

I have just won gold in the 'Flinging a supplement across the room' event.

Steve Brown
London SW6

SIR – Why are you the only national newspaper which never wishes its readers a happy new year? Hiding it in the puzzle reaches only a proportion of your readers.

Alan Varley-Largo
Crowborough, East Sussex

SIR — I was writing in the third clue for your quick crossword just after eleven o'clock this morning when the announcer on Radio 4 said the answer: 'Evelyn Waugh'. How's that for serendipity? But she could have told me earlier.

Audrey Buxton
Greetham, Rutland

PALTROWED BY THE PICTURE EDITOR

SIR — Breakfast this morning was disturbed by a vocal rumble from the other end of the table. I was happily reading Mandrake when came the cry: 'We're being Paltrowed again!'

Much as I abhor the creation of silly new verbs, it didn't take me long to discover the source of my wife's displeasure. It was yet another banner photograph of the fragrant Miss Paltrow on the front of the *Telegraph*.

What is going on? I realise that the world's most beautiful woman has some sort of cookbook coming out, but this media onslaught over the past month really is unnerving.

Might I suggest we go back to the days when Gwyneth didn't cook — the *ante*-Paltrow era, perhaps? This is not to be confused with the *anti*-

Paltrow position, i.e. those who think the timbre of Gwyneth's voice has much in common with a 20cc Chinese chainsaw.

Stephen Lewis
Wirral

SIR – Have I missed something? Please can someone tell me who James Middleton is, and what he is doing in a newspaper? My husband has a blue suit – can I send in a photo?

Celia Smith
Wilton, Wiltshire

SIR – Does the editor of *The Daily Telegraph* fancy Pippa Middleton? If not, why do we have so many photos of that woman?

Roy France
Billinge, Merseyside

SIR – I'm sure this won't be printed, but I'd love to know your mindset on a 'celebrity' who in her book regards cushions on sofas as 'funky' at Christmas.

Pippa Middleton is a lovely girl, but today's paper shows her applauding at a tennis match. Is that all you can come up with? How pathetic is that?

Walter Walker
Holtye Common, Kent

SIR — A year ago I gave up buying *The Daily Telegraph* because I was bored by the daily picture of Pippa Middleton. Now that I have decided to resubscribe, I have become bored by the daily picture of Clare Balding.

Simon Payton
Malvern, Worcestershire

SIR — Is Amanda Thatcher the new Pippa Middleton?

Lieutenant Commander P.J. Barber (retd)
Norton Juxta Twycross, Warwickshire

SIR — I was about to complain that I was getting withdrawal symptoms because you haven't published a photograph of Helen Mirren or the Duchess of Cambridge for at least two days, but then you surpass yourselves with three pictures of the actress on page seven.

Martin Vousden
Friockheim, Angus

SIR — I am sure that I am not alone in noticing that in almost every Business section of the *Telegraph*, a photo of a beautiful woman appears on page three. This is not a complaint.

Nicholas Carson
Birlingham, Worcestershire

SIR — Today's *Telegraph* is the most annoying ever.
Full of fashion photographs and, astonishingly,
a repeat of the photographs of French female
politicians. I realise they are much better looking
than our lot, but once is surely enough.

   Alright, I'm grumpy and 83 but there are a lot
of us around — and, according to reports, we are
growing in number. Watch it!

Kel Prince
Rothley, Leicestershire

SIR — Pictures of men in mini-skirts and kinky
boots very nearly spoiled my breakfast today.
My choking fit calmed down when I got to the
photograph of Miss Alabama on Page 15. The
picture editor really must bear in mind the health
of old men.

T.W.
Barnham, West Sussex

SIR — Is the reason Denise Garrido, the short-
lived Miss Canada, didn't last very long because she
appears to have the word *penis* spelled on her sash?

Jeremy Burton
Shurlock Row, Berkshire

SIR – Why on earth does the food pictured on
the Sunday Lunch Club page always look like dog
vomit? And incidentally, what an appalling way to
serve that king of meats, venison.

Nick Allen
Adderbury, Oxfordshire

HAM SANDWICH

SIR – I would be delighted to think that Mr Billy
Gammon and Miss Michelle Trotter, whose
engagement is announced in the *Telegraph* today, were
first attracted to each other by the coincidence of
their surnames. We should all wish them well.

Juliet Dettmer
Hambledon, Hampshire

THE BURGLAR SECTION

SIR – I was intrigued to read in today's Property
section the following sentence describing the charms
of a house for sale: 'To keep valuables out of sight,
there is a safe and a gun locker hidden behind a
bookcase in the living room.'

Nigel Burdett
Kelsale, Suffolk

THE DAILY MATT

SIR — Is there any way I can get Matt, daily,
without 30 pages of impending disaster and those
damnable adverts?

Chris Beale
Wells-next-the-Sea, Norfolk

SIR — When is the incomparable Matt going to be
awarded his knighthood? His cartoon today made
me choke over my morning coffee. This wonderful
self-effacing man deserves to be recognised.

Chrissie Carling
Brokenborough, Wiltshire

SIR — A while ago the Mayan calendar predicted the
imminent end of civilisation as we know it. How we
laughed. Now I discover that both Matt and Alex are
on holiday. Maybe, just maybe, the Mayans knew
more than they were letting on.

Stewart Lock
Crawley, West Sussex

PS

SIR — I recently obtained a copy of *I Rest My Case*....
One letter contained the words 'manky badger'.
I would like to look at that letter again but am
unable to find it. I've scanned the book twice
more. Can you help?

David Chinn
Issaquah, WA, USA

Dear David (if I may),
But of course — the phrase appears on page 174
in a letter from a Cornish cyclist complaining
about the things he passes on his daily
40-mile commute.
    Kind regards,

Iain Hollingshead

Dear Iain (you may),
Thanks for replying. In America, 'manky' is
unknown to nearly everyone; of approximately
30 friends of mine, only one had heard of the word.
They all like it, however. 'Manky badger' rolls off
the tongue effortlessly. Much like 'cheeky bastard',
one friend said.
    I think it's a name in search of a cocktail.
A manly cocktail — perhaps involving a bitter of
some sort. Certainly those four syllables could be

easily understood and heard in the noisiest of bars.
　Warm regards,

　　　David Chinn
　　　Issaquah, WA, USA

Dear Mr Hollingshead,
Your letter informing me that I might have the
honour of appearing in *Am I Missing Something…?*
made my day if not my life. This is an unexpected
honour and a million times better than
remembering that I inadvertently,
but wisely, refused a Tesco meat pie at a party.
　Do make sure that the Library of Congress
in America gets a copy as they have a slight
misunderstanding of British humour. I am sure
a small volume like this will go some way to
amending the situation.

　　　Loris Goring
　　　Brixham, Devon

Dear Mr Hollingshead,
Of course I do not mind you using my earlier
missive in a fresh edition of your splendid annual
compendium – if only to prove to one of my sons,
who buys it, that I am still alive.

　　　Rear Admiral J.A.L. Myres
　　　Dorchester-on-Thames, Oxfordshire